MURAQABA

MURAQABA

The Art and Science
of
Sufi Meditation

By
Shaykh
Khwaja Shamsuddin Azeemi
Patriarch
of the Sufi Order of Azeemia

Translated by:
Syed Shahzad Reaz

Plato Publishing, Inc.
Houston, Texas

Published By:
Plato Publishing, Inc.
3262 Westheimer Rd 258
Houston TX 77098

Library of Congress Catalog Card Number: 2004095647

ISBN:0-9758875-4-8
First Edition: January 2005

Designed and Produced by:
Kingsley Literary Services, Ltd
2656 South Loop West, Suite 440
Houston, Texas 77054
www.bookdesigns.net

Contents

Chapter   *Page*

Introduction vii
About the Author xii
From the Translator's Desk xiv
1. Self and the Cosmos 1
2. Mental Concentration 4
3. Spiritual Brain 9
4. Waves of Thought 13
5. Third Eye 16
6. Film and Screen 20
7. Motions of the Spirit 23
8. Electrical System 29
9. Three Layers 33
10. Heart of the Cosmos 37
11. Concept of Unity 40
12. Muraqaba and Religion 42
13. Benefits of Muraqaba 57
14. Levels 61
15. Subtle Sensations 74
16. Spiritual Journey 88
17. Fatah (Exploration) 91
18. Classification of Muraqaba 97
19. Helpful Excercises 108
20. 16-Week Program 112
21. Spiritual Concept of Healing 116
22. Muraqaba of Colored Lights 117
23. Station of Ihsaan 125

Chapter *Page*

24. The Hidden World 128
25. Muraqaba of Life After Death 131
26. Kashaf ul Qaboor 138
27. Dress of Soul 142
28. Haatif Ghaybi 145
29. Tassawar Shaykh 154
30. Tassawar Rasul 156
31. Divine Essence 157
    Glossary 159
    Suggested Reading 163
    Index 167

Introduction

By

Shaykh Khwaja Shamsuddin Azeemi
Khanuadah,
Silsila-e-Aaliya Azeemia

When we try to learn a new skill or try to gain knowledge about a specific subject, we follow a guideline or a system, which demands that we pay attention to the subject to fully understand it. Our mind becomes curious to know the where, how and what of it. When we pay attention to the minor details, that minor point itself gains value. However, when we ignore the most important part and do not pay any cognitive attention to it then even that major point loses its value and importance. Through contemplation we gain knowledge about any object and the deeper that knowledge the more we learn about that object and its qualities.

Muraqaba is the name of that contemplation (*tafakkur*) through which man is able to gain the knowledge (*ilm*) which is the primordial knowledge of his Ego, Self, or Soul. After gaining that knowledge, any man can gain access to his Ego or Soul.

It appears that the person performing Muraqaba is simply sitting in a pose with his or her eyes closed. However, merely shutting the eyes and assuming a specific pose does not serve the purpose. Muraqaba is in fact an angle of perception (*tarz-e-fikr*) through which the person doing the Muraqaba frees himself or herself from outward (*zahir*) senses and begins their journey in the inward (*batin*) senses.

Now we are going to look into whether or not the Muraqaba-like conditions or states exist in us, without adopting the specific pose of Muraqaba.

Freedom from outward senses happens in our daily life, both involuntarily and voluntarily. For example, we go to sleep and while sleeping our brain disconnects from outward senses. It is true that this disconnection is temporary however; this condition could not be termed as anything but disconnection from outward senses. Hence, we can say that Muraqaba is in fact a way of imposing a state of sleeping without going to sleep.

Every human being, from the time of birth to their death spends life in two states. In other words, in the human mind there are two types of

vii

conditions that prevail every moment of our life. One of these conditions or states is wakening and the other sleeping or dreaming. In the wakening state, they are trapped in Time and Space while during dreaming they are free from the confines of spatiotemporal limitations. This freedom of Time and Space is sought through Muraqaba by converting the state of sleeping or dreaming into an awakened state. Because during Muraqaba, a person goes through the same conditions that he or she goes through while sleeping or dreaming.

The notion that dreams are nothing but thoughts is not correct. In all scriptures including the *Qur'an* (Koran), dreams have been mentioned. The dreams that were mentioned in the *Qur'an* show that the realm of dream is free from the restrictions imposed by Time and Space. When a person tries to impose the state of dreaming through Muraqaba, they free themselves from that spatiotemporal boundaries and they journey through the realm of dream the way they travel while fully wake. All existing things need foundation; without it they could not survive. This is not something that is hard to comprehend. For example the foundation of a chair is its legs. A house remains erect only when inside the earth its foundation is laid. Similarly, we can only learn a subject or a branch of knowledge when we know its basics. These basics (or formulas) are considered as the foundation of any branch of knowledge. God has revealed it in the *Qur'an*,

"Al-Lah is the light (*nur*) of the heavens and earth."

In this Universe, there are several worlds and galaxies. The Essence and Reality of God is something only God knows or those with whom He has shared His Secrets. How much of this information God has shared with His chosen servants is not our concern. However, we do know that God created this entire universe for us humans. It is stated on several occasions in the Qur'an that the foundation of this universe is the Light (*nur*) of God. Based on this fact it is imperative that Man and all of his abilities be centered on one foundation.

It is our daily observation that not all of our actions, motions, whims, thoughts, imaginations, and feelings are dependent on the body of bones and flesh. Because when the Spirit disconnects its link with the physical body then this body of bones and flesh is unable to act on its own. As long as the Spirit is attached with the body, all the needs, and functions necessary for life are present. In other words, Spirit (*ruh*) is the foundation of the body.

According to the Qur'an, a limited knowledge of the Spirit is given. Nevertheless even this limited knowledge is still knowledge. What we are trying to emphasize is that what we consider Man is a body of bones and flesh, though that Man is nothing but fiction. The real Man is the one that protects that skeleton of flesh and keeps it in motion, whom the Qur'an calls *ruh* (Spirit). This *ruh,* in order to fulfill the needs of life uses a medium. We call this medium chromosomes. In the Qur'an, God has said that, "We poured Our *ruh* in him (Adam)." In other words, *ruh* created a medium and after that gave him the senses. *Ruh* is in fact a component of the Divine and in it all the knowledge (*ilm*) of Divine Discretions (*mashiat*) and Attributes (*sifat*) are present, which God so Willed. Just how this knowledge was acquired by the component, is a Divine Mystery, which could never be explained.

There are eleven thousand generators (*latifa,* plural *lataif*) at work inside man. According to Sufism, there are eleven thousand Divine Names as well. Every Divine Name is an Attribute (*sifat*) and every Divine Attribute is knowledge (*ilm*). This knowledge further expands into more and more spheres to become a manifestation of the Divine Attributes.

In order to enter the unseen world (*a'lam al-ghayb*) or to behold anything beyond Time and Space, we have to first free ourselves from the clutches of spatiotemporal restrictions. This is only possible when the vision that sees Time and Space frees itself from its boundaries. To activate that vision, certain exercises have been created through which even if the human mind is not totally free at least it is able to come close to it.

Now the next question is how and when the human senses could be freed from that restriction. One example is the state of dreaming. Sleeping actually is getting freedom from the diurnal senses, which are Time and Space. When we go to sleep then our senses are transferred to a realm where the state of Time and Space do exist but not in the chronological order in which we spend our life. The Second way is that while wake human mind could focus on any object with full concentration. For example when we read an interesting book, we often lost track of the time. When we finally look at our watch, we then realize that so much time has elapsed, though we were not aware of it.

In the *Qur'an*, the event of Moses receiving the Torah is mentioned in the following verse,

"And We promised Moses thirty nights and fulfilled it in forty nights."

Day and night are mentioned in the *Qur'an* in the following verses,

"And We enter night into the day and let the day enter into the night."
"We take the night out of the day and take the day out of the night."
"We cover the day onto night and night into the day..."

When we contemplate these verses of the *Qur'an*, we realized that day and night are in fact two senses. In other words, our life is divided into two senses. One of the senses is day the other one is night. During the day senses (diurnal senses) restricted with Time and Space while during night senses (nocturnal senses) we are free from these restrictions.

The Divine Statement, "We promised Moses thirty nights and fulfilled it in forty nights" is interesting. Because Moses did not simply spend forty nights there, his entire stay was forty days *and* forty nights. It was not that he was spending the nights at the place and coming back during the day. He did spend his entire stay at the Mount. Interestingly God did not mention days in the verse instead mentions only night. It clearly suggests that during those forty days and forty nights, Moses was under the influence of nocturnal senses, the same nocturnal senses which free us from the restrictions of Time and Space.

Hence, anyone who would impose the nocturnal senses during the period of day and night on themselves would be free from the confinement of Time and Space. This freedom from spatiotemporal restriction is the way to exploring the unseen realm (*a'lam al-ghayb*) and getting intuitive information.

During a battle, an arrow injured Imam Ali. It had entered his thigh and the pain was excruciating. The surgeons could not operate on it. Because of extreme pain he would not let them even touch it. One of his companions suggested to the surgeons that they wait until Imam Ali began his prayer. When Imam Ali began his prayer, the surgeons were able to operate on him without him showing any sign of pain. By the time he was done with his prayers, Imam Ali realized that the surgeon had already performed the surgery and the wound had already been stitched. This event is another example of the negation of Time and Space. When Imam Ali started his prayers, his senses went from diurnal state into nocturnal state. The moment his mind entered the nocturnal senses his focus was shifted away from the diurnal senses (restriction and pain). The foundation of Spirituality is based on the reality that Man has two senses, two brains, and two lives. Just like the two sides of a coin, it has two sides. One life is restricted; the other one is free. Constrained life is day, wakefulness, and consciousness. On the other hand, free life is the name of night, joy, peace and the contentment of the heart.

To gain that life the easiest method in Spirituality is Muraqaba. Muraqaba is in fact the name of an exercise, effort and the angle of perception. Through it, anyone can enter the nocturnal senses while keeping the diurnal senses active as well. Since entering from diurnal senses to nocturnal senses is not something that he is used to or familiar with, in the beginning he faces challenges. This could become a burden on the consciousness and sometimes results in nervous breakdowns or other mental disorders. To avoid that situation, a person or teacher is needed who has gone through the different stages of learning and is quite familiar with the ups and down of it. This teacher would protect the student from any over-load on the consciousness. This learned and experienced teacher is called the *shaykh* (Sufi Master), *pir,* or *murshid*. The person who receives that training is referred as *murid*.

Allahum'ma lakal hamdu wa' lakal shukr
(Praise and thankfulness be to God).

About the Author

Born Khwaja Shamsuddin Ansari on October 17, 1927 in Siharanpur, U.P., India into a radical Sunni cleric household; young Shamsuddin saw firsthand the superficiality of the legalistic outward religion. Growing up he had several encounters that provoked his interests in the esoteric religion. At the young age of twenty, he set out on the quest of finding a true *murshid* (Sufi Master). That nine-year journey took him from his native city to places like the Patiala State, India and then to Lahore and then to Sadiqabad, Pakistan. Finally in Karachi, he arrived at the doorsteps of the Syed Muhammad Azeem a.k.a. Qalandar Baba Awliya (1896-1979), founder of the Sufi Order of Azeemia and grandson of the famous Indian Sufi, Baba Tajuddin of Nagpur (1852?-1929).

The next fourteen years under his tutelage saw the transformation of this undereducated and functionally illiterate person into the author of around a dozen books and several articles on parapsychology, telepathy, and spirituality. In 1962, Shaykh Azeemi started writing articles on spirituality in various Pakistani newspapers and magazines. The most famous of them was his advice column Roohani Daak, in *Urdu Daily Jung*. People from all walks of life and faith would write to him for his advice on their problems. On average, Shaykh Azeemi received 3,000 mails a day. Because of its huge success, a monthly magazine *Roohani Digest* was launched in 1978. Shaykh Azeemi is the Editor in Chief of the magazine, which now has its own website www.roohanidigest.com. In 1979 before his physical death, Qalandar Baba Awliya designated Shaykh Azeemi as the Patriarch of the Sufi Order of Azeemia.

What sets this Sufi Order apart from most of the other Orders is that it is available to people from all the faiths. Hence, a number of Shaykh Azeemi's students are Hindus, Christians and Zoroastrian as well as members of other faiths. The main headquarters of the Sufi Order of Azeemia is its convent (*khanqah*) at Surjani Town, subdivision of Karachi, where Shaykh Azeemi still receives and gives free advice to people daily. The convent holds weekly Muraqaba sessions as well as training classes and *lungar*.

Since 2001, Shaykh Azeemi has delegated most of his editorial responsibilities to his eldest son and *shaykh*-designate Mr. Waqar

Yousuf Azeemi. Mr. Waqar Yousuf Azeemi, himself an author, was recently elected the Finance-Secretary of the prestigious All-Pakistan Newspaper Society (APNS), an organization credited with upholding and striving for the freedom of the press in that country.

— **Syed Shahzad Reaz**

From The Translator's Desk

I have been a fan of Shaykh Azeemi's writing since my teen years. Early on when I observed the hypocrisy and shallowness of the religious establishment and was growing tired of the rhetoric, his writings on metaphysics, on parapsychology as well as other social evils facing the Muslims Societies were a breath of fresh air. His approach was very different; instead of being overly critical or self-righteous, he always offered hope, introduced new ideas and optimism. The first time that I attended the Urs ceremony of Qalandar Baba Awliya (1896-1979) in Karachi was in 1990, I noticed that toward the end of the ceremony people, young and old, male and female would line up just to get a hug from the Shaykh. You could see their anxiousness as they wait their turn. In a culture of least physical contact, where even parents do not hug their adult children and public display of affection is limited to very young children, that too was refreshing. Back then I was only familiar with his writing and have not yet met the Shaykh in person. So I too joined the queue. After a long wait , in which people of different economic and ethnic backgrounds and from different parts of the world formed a single line, got their hug, some cried on his shoulder, some asked him to pray for them, I too got my turn. I then realized why people were waiting so anxiously for so long. It was a very brief hug but I felt something. It wasn't that I hadn't hugged anyone before but this was different.

Shaykh Azeemi has since transformed many lives through his writings and his teaching of spiritual awareness. When this book Muraqaba first came out in Urdu, I almost had this urge that this book in particular need to be translated into English. Fortunately, the Shaykh on his last visit to Houston granted me the permission to translate it.

Anyone who has written or translated a book knows that it is not a one man job. It is indeed a team effort. I could not have translated this book without the support, encouragements, and advice of countless friends and well-wishers. First, I would like to thank Dr. Harold Raley for the excellent editing and David Raley of Kingsley Literary Services for the cover design and layout setup. I could not have done without you. To Dr. Carl W. Ernst, Author and Professor of University of North Carolina at Chapel Hill for his advise on uniformity of using the Sufi terms. To Shaykh Kabir Helminski for his kind words for the project. To

Syed M Azhar, founder of Sheikh Chilli Restaurant of Houston, the first and only Pakistani-restaurant in the city back in 70's and a popular local radio personality, for his encouragements throughout the project. Mr. Azhar is definitely the icon of the South Asian community of Houston. I would also like to thank Brother Abdul Hafeez Butt of Manchester, England, who last year lost his wife and life companion Syeda Saeeda Khatoon, yet gracefully assisted in the project. To Naseem Burke of New Orleans and Rashida Jilani of Toronto, Canada, both in charge of their local chapters of Azeemi Order for wishing the project well. To Fasahat Mohiuddin of Modern Tribune and to Urdu literary society of Houston, Gahwar-e-Adab's Attorney Syed Nayyer Izfar, Syed Mohsin Zaidi, Arslan Usmani, Syed Ameerul Hasan, former labor leader Ghulam Mohyuddin Chisti, Imtiaz Ahsan, Aman Khan, Aijaz Ahmed, Khalid Ali, Shoaib Ahmed, Syed Athar Ali Kazmi, Moidul Hasan, Ali Hasan, Azam Akhtar, City Councilman M J Khan and HPD officer Muzaffar Siddiqi and to Mr. Ashraf Meghani of J&M for taking care of most of my accounting and other related paper-work and to Mian Nazir of Rehmania for his kind wishes as well and to anyone I missed, I apologize in advance. I thank all of you for your support and kind words.

Last but not least, I would like to show my gratitude for Shaykh Azeemi for entrusting me with this task and giving me the permission to translate his book and to God for giving me the ability to do and complete this job.

1

Self and the Cosmos

In the current information age, the very question of what Man is, and to what extent his abilities go, has gained prominence. Metaphysical knowledge tells us that Man is not just a mass of muscles and bones but in fact is a living universe or microcosm (*a'lam asghar*) itself. His life is primarily relying on information. As a matter of fact his life is nothing but a collection of thoughts and imagination. His every movement is influenced by information and thoughts. Every human achievement is circled around the unseen world of cognition, imagination and creative thoughts. By giving new meaning to this idea, Man creates and invents new things out of nothing.

Human consciousness has evolved in a way similar to child development. From day one to around age five, a child's cognitive abilities remain marginal, and from age six to pre-puberty their mental ability improves to a degree. However, after puberty and adolescence, when they enter adulthood, their mental and physical abilities reach its zenith. In a similar fashion, human consciousness has also developed itself slowly to its modern or current level. Although the modern world has developed and is advanced technologically, it would be presumptuous to think that the time we are living in has achieved its highest level of knowledge and inventiveness. Human mind has an unlimited potential to grow and expand without ever being stopped at any given point. The truth is that there exists a huge chunk of discoveries and explorations that is still hidden or simply beyond the scope of the human mind. Mind is the basis of all experiments, observations and senses. No human inventions could be possible without it. During the cognitive process, the mind expands its capabilities and as a result innovations and new branches of knowledge emerge. Human mind has always been a mystery for thousands of years up to our present age. Scientists believe that we have only consumed five to ten percent of our mental capabilities. A much larger share of its strength is still lying dormant. In other words what we have achieved so far is only five to ten percent of our hidden mental capability.

What we have discussed so far shows that current explorations and developments in the fields of medicine, Botany and Zoology, Genetics, Physics, Chemistry, Architecture, Psychology and Parapsychology and other areas reflect human capabilities. However we rarely come to this conclusion that all these are actually mirroring our mental abilities which the Nature has given to us.

Every day discoveries about the mind and *inner dimensions* are showing that human existence is divided into two. One half is its outer layer and the second half is the movement in its *inner plane*. These two sides are linked with each other. The idea that Man is not simply confined to his physical side and outward feelings has surfaced from time to time in all phases of human history. There is an internal sphere in humans which is independent of material needs. This is the sphere that is behind sending the entire cognitive stimulus to the physical sphere. That internal sphere is actually what Man is and is commonly known as the Soul *(nafas)* or Spirit *(ruh)*. Spiritualists of all times have maintained that if we focus on our *inner* or spiritual heart, we would be able to explore the might or the potential of our true Self.

All revealed scriptures have generally mentioned the paranormal capabilities of human. According to them, outwardly, human beings are made of bones and flesh but in their *inner self* lies energy, which is the reflection of the attributes of their Creator. This is what Spirit *(ruh)* is. Through this energy, the spiritual person receives the Divine Knowledge.

Revealed scriptures have divided the human senses in two major spheres: the Cosmos *(macrocosm)* and the Self *(microcosm)*. The Cosmos *(a'alm akbar)* represents all outward physical or material beings and the Self *(a'lam asghar)* is everything that exists within. The human knowledge about the Self or *inner being* is at the initial phase right now. Just as a few hundred years back, most scientific knowledge of today would have been considered witchcraft or magic but are now part of our everyday life. In the same respect, the knowledge regarding the Self is at its infancy level right now. We are only beginning to know the wonders and depths of it.

Vision, Hearing, Speech, Taste and Touch are usually considered as the basic five senses of human being. Each one is well defined and has its own application. Similarly, each one has its own limits as well. For instance we are not able to see objects beyond a certain distance, or are unable to hear voices under a certain frequency or could not touch anything unless it is within our physical reach.

All five of these senses have limits within the physical realm but they are limitless in the spiritual realm. The spiritual senses usually remain hidden or dormant. However once they are activated the vision becomes independent of any boundaries or confinement of distance. The ear hears sounds of any wavelength and speech no longer finds itself in need of any words. Without uttering a single word a person could send or receive his or her thoughts to anyone, anytime no matter where the subject is. The truth is that human senses actually come to their peak when spiritual senses are in motion. These senses open the door for such limitless observations and explorations that are normally dormant. Through these senses alone, a person could enter the hidden realm of millions of galaxies and countless stars and could encounter creatures that are otherwise considered non-existent such as angels or species of other planets.

The most effective way of activating and enhancing the spiritual sense is **Muraqaba** (meditation). Muraqaba is an exercise, a skill, or simply a way of thinking, which turns the otherwise dormant senses into a vibrant and awake mode. Through it we can explore those forces that are beyond the scope of physical senses. It also serves to improve the already existing paranormal abilities of an individual. Throughout human history it has existed in one form or the other.

Spiritually and psychologically as well as physiologically there are various advantages of practicing Muraqaba. First and foremost it improves concentration, immunity, memory, prevents psychological complications, and controls our negative thoughts and emotions thereby giving us a feeling of serenity and tranquility. Overall we are able to perform well in our daily tasks whether it is work related or in relationships.

The basic element of Muraqaba exists in all major religions of the world in one way or the other. Emphasis on prayer is always placed on higher focus and deeper thinking. So far in this chapter we have discussed the Muraqaba in general. However in the following chapters we are going to discuss the different forms of Muraqaba and its classification. We will briefly shed some light on other spiritual exercises, as well as ways to activate and improve the hidden capabilities vis-a-vis the spiritual powers of our relatively unknown self.

2

Mental Concentration

In our material life we have various abilities to perform different tasks. All of these are the abilities of the conscious mind. For example the ability to touch, to feel, to listen, to smell, to behold, to taste, to speak, to hold, to walk, to sleep or to arise and so on all fall under that category. Various branches of knowledge like art, music, printing, literature, poetry, history, science and so on and so forth are also in the same league. When someone wants to learn a skill that he or she does not already know, the first thing they need to do is to concentrate on the idea of learning that particular skill and then depending on their overall enthusiasm, the hidden qualities and abilities come to the surface. Bottom line is that to set any ability into motion the primary thing is to focus on it. No one could acquire any skill or ability without concentrating on the idea of acquiring that skill. Whether it is intentional or unintentional, concentration is the basis of all learning and acquiring new skills.

This rule also applies to the awakening of spiritual abilities. Since we are unaware of the extent of our spiritual potential, we simply do not even attempt to focus on it. Unless someone would try to focus on his or her *inner self*, their spiritual abilities would never emerge.

We all know for a fact that unless any work is done using the full concentration, desired results would never be achieved. Whether it is educational, sports or spiritual, mental concentration is the backbone of all the achievements. To learn something we need an environment where there is least distraction. When we learn something new using full concentration, we usually achieve the desired results. On the other hand if the environment is full of distraction then our objective could not be achieved, no matter great our ability to learn it.

Concentration is the name of focusing the mind into one point so that it could be focused on a single thought or point. Through it, the scattered forces from the depth of mind converge and then surface. The reason why so many reflections of the soul and its unlimited force remain dormant is because the power of mental concentration is hardly used to activate the paranormal capabilities that exist within each of us.

4

Under the influence of emotions, thoughts, and urges, the mind is constantly changing from one state to the other. It never stays in a single state. Due to the constant influx of thoughts, we failed to perceive the stations that are the source of our origin.

Example

Radio stations throughout the world relay their transmission on the air through radio waves. Each wave has its own frequency. The various radio sets receiving the transmission are receivers, because they receive the transmission. To receive those transmissions radio sets must be tuned to the same frequency, which is the frequency of that radio station. It is our daily routine that whenever we want to hear our favorite radio station, all we have to do is to adjust the switch to the relaying station's frequency. When the receiving frequency corresponds to the relaying frequency we start hearing our favorite station.

All radio stations relay their programming in different frequencies. When the frequencies do not match, we do not hear anything. In the same way if there is resistance of any kind, for example bad weather, we do not hear the clear sound. In case of television sound and picture are relayed together. We not only hear the sound but watch the pictures as well in different channels.

In the same way human consciousness is also a receiver. The information that is stored in the depth of the mind transmits itself in various forms to the consciousness. Some information is displayed in the form of pictures, some in the form of imagination. Others are received in the form of thought, while some are also received as sound.

We all know for a fact that thoughts come to our mind involuntarily. There is not a single moment in our life when we are free of thoughts. What we do not realize is the urges for food and water to end our hunger and thirst are also thoughts. And so are our needs for sleep or awakening after sleep. Happiness, sadness, and other emotions are thoughts as well. Not only thoughts and imaginations but vision, hearing, touch are nothing but information. In fact our whole life revolves around thoughts and when this process finally ends, it culminates in death.

Law of Inventions

When a thought goes deeper, it has a way of manifesting itself. If life were something other than the thoughts then they would not have affected us. However, the truth is that when happier thoughts come to our mind, we feel serenity and peace. Scary thoughts make us fearful and when doubts enter our mind, we become anxious. From the medical point of view, this has been recognized as well. Diseases and disorders like ulcers, other digestive ailments, hypertension, depression and others either are caused or get complicated by thoughts. This is our daily observation that when we are worried or anxious, we lose our appetite. Even a remote thought about an accident or any other disaster could send our heart rate up. In the same way, we would not be able to go to work or school unless the thought of going to work or school enters our conscious mind. For instance if we wanted to build a house, the first thought that comes to our mind is the need of the house. When this thought activates we start making plans for it like getting the capital or loan, contact builders and so on. The architecture itself is stored in the human mind in the form of a thought. Therefore, when the forces of thoughts and action combine, the construction of the house starts. The house that once existed in the form of a thought manifests itself into a building.

The scriptures tell us that there is a single source of all the thoughts. That source is the Point of Self (*nuqta dhat*) which exists in the depths of the mind. Through this source, unlimited information (thought) is transmitted continuously. However, the information that is received by the conscious receiver is very limited. This information becomes his knowledge and memory and it is this, which we call consciousness. To receive more and detailed information we need to have higher mental concentration. When our cognition descends into our Point of Self with full mental focus, then little by little we encounter that information that is beyond the scope of our ordinary senses.

The last boundary of this transmitting information is really what consciousness is all about. To receive more and in-depth information, we have to be acquainted with our subconscious. Just as in the field of science, any new formula or invention is in fact new information. Scientists and inventors spend days, months, and sometimes years on contemplating on a point; this cognitive activity eventually sends them into the realm of subconscious that exists beyond the layers of consciousness. This results in the discovery or invention of something new. Therefore, even they could not come to any conclusion unless they venture into the subconscious.

First, the idea about an invention enters the mind of the inventor and his mind starts to focus on it. The deeper the mind descends into the thought, the greater the thought broadens; and the form and figures of that thought begin to form. Eventually it manifests as the final invention. Here we can use the invention of airplanes as an example. First in the human mind, the very idea of flight came by simply watching the birds. That curiosity or the desire to fly in space continued to guide man over time. When one generation died, it gave away its conscious inheritance to the new generation. First, humans tried to imitate the birds by attaching wings to their bodies, but that did not work. Nevertheless, that failure did not stop the desire and so the process continued for centuries. Some like Leonardo Da Vinci came very close but the end product was still far away. Little by little, the mechanics of flight started to emerge in the mind and the concepts of air pressure and aerodynamics were finally revealed. And as we know it, the Wright brothers finally succeeded in making a machine that could fly and the rest is history.

All branches of knowledge, rational or intuitive, work the same way. That is, when the mind focuses on any given idea or topic with all its abilities then hidden details leap into the mind. When the cognition focuses on the outward or physical subjects, then physical knowledge is revealed and when it descends into the *inner plane* then esoteric knowledge and revelation surface.

The consciousness of a child is different from that of an adult. At the time of the birth, the child is unaware of his environment. His vision hardly stays on any object nor could he comprehend the sounds around his environment. He could not speak or sense time and space. Slowly and gradually, he learns more or less everything that is prevalent in his environment (i.e., society). Even the way of thinking is transferred from his environment to him. In this transfer, the child's will or intention also plays a part. A big chunk of knowledge that he receives comes involuntarily from the people of his environment. He learns to speak his native language without ever receiving a formal education for that language. In the same way, he learns the meaning and use of the objects present in his environment. More or less a child sees, understands, and perceives the knowledge and consciousness of his elders. By the time he reaches adulthood, his consciousness contains roughly everything that enables him to lead the life in the same manner or style that is prevalent in his society.

To better explain consciousness we can use the example of a mirror. On it the lights fall and reflect, in the same way thoughts in the form of lights shine on consciousness and based on its knowledge and interest, it absorbs some of those while letting go of others. The lights that the consciousness absorbs stay on the screen. Man sees and feels them but those that cross its screen he is able to behold.

Example

If a clear, clean glass is placed in front of you, and you are unaware of it then you would not be able to see it. The reason is simple, the light passes through that glass, and reflection does not occur. Since there is no reflection, eyes could not see it. You might have seen people would walk towards those glass walls and only after they are hit with it that they realize that it was a glass.

The consciousness has a natural ability that when it is focused on an object, it starts absorbing the lights from it. These lights, which were then unknown, become declassified, as it gets hold of them. This hold or grasp is what we call knowledge, experience, and observation etc.

According to the Spiritual branch of knowledge, the unseen realm holds an unlimited number of these lights. In this realm of lights lie the galaxies, the species of other planets, civilizations, and spiritual mysteries and abundance of spiritual knowledge. When you shift your focus to your inner Self then on the screen of your consciousness is information that starts to appear in the form of images and your consciousness is then able to understand them as they appear. Gradually it understands and feels them just as a child slowly gets acquainted with his environment.

The will or intention plays a big part in activating your spiritual or hidden senses. When you do Muraqaba with your closed eyes, you are aware that beyond this darkness those objects do exist. This awareness helps activate your esoteric vision. At first, you get frustrated but with continued practice, your will or intention is set into motion and you with your eyes closed are able to see the unseen realm just as with open eyes you see the material world.

We all know that belief plays a major part in achieving anything. If you do not believe that New York is a city then you would never be able to get there. If we do not believe in Chemistry as a science, we would not able to learn it. Ever.

3
Spiritual Brain

Many life experiences and events point to the fact that there are perceptual resources available besides the physical senses in humans whose capability and attributes are much higher and greater than normal senses. Based on the way with which these perceptual resources are exposed to us, different terms have been assigned to them, for example sixth sense, Extra Sensory Perception or ESP, intuition, conscience, inner voice and spiritual flight among others.

We all go through a certain phase of our life when the ability to think becomes clogged. We cannot make up our mind in the face of turmoil or a crisis. In the midst of that confusion, a thought suddenly crosses our mind like a flash and we become aware of something that could not be explained, nor does it have any apparent relationship to the state of affairs. This thought is sometimes so strong that we simply cannot avoid being influenced by it. The more compelling fact is that when we act on that very thought, the problem that we were facing, goes away. Often we hear people saying that their sixth sense was telling them something or that they were receiving a thought repeatedly and then it all happened the way it was in their mind.

Example I:

You suddenly start thinking about a relative whom you have not seen in years. From time to time, his or her picture appears in your mind though there is no apparent reason for it. You began questioning yourself why it was happening. Sometimes it may also be accompanied by feelings of happiness or of worry. Shortly thereafter, you learn that same person either is sick or was involved in an accident. In the same way sometimes a thought of a friend starts coming into your mind for no reason and moments later same person is knocking at your door. Often when a group of people is talking about something and the topic of discussion imperceptibly moves to an absent specific person and a short while later, that same person shows up unexpectedly.

9

Example II:

A scientist spends time researching something and analyzing the results and during that process of deep thinking, he or she is able to form a new idea. This new discovery would then become the basis for a new formula or a branch of science. This discovery process unfolds in a step-by-step way or in some occasions bypasses all the trial and error stages and forms in an instant. In a step-by-step process, this discovery does not feel to be out of ordinary. However if it happened in an instant then it cannot be termed as the working of the normal senses.

In organic chemistry Benzene is a compound. The discovery of its molecular structure is in many ways similar to what we have just discussed. Chemist Friedrich August Kekulé (1829-1896) was busy finding out the molecular structure of Benzene, since based on earlier assumptions it was not what he thought it should have been. However, even after spending day after day he was not able to come to any conclusion. One night he saw in his dream that there were six serpents who were grabbing each other's tail in such a way that it formed a specific figure. Simply by looking at that figure he got the idea of the molecular structure of Benzene. After he woke up, he worked on that figure for a while and proved that the molecular structure of Benzene is the same as what he had seen in his dream.

In the same way, many advances in the field of medicine are a result of intuitive guidance. Because of mental work of the doctors and or researchers, the mind focuses on any chemical, compound, or drug and through experiments and research the intuitive signal is transformed into the material form and figure and the belief of its success.

Creative art as well as any other conscious performance is also influenced by the delicate perception. Many subjects, writings, poems, and thoughts cannot be viewed as cognitive efforts. This is also noted by authors, painters, poets, or philosophers and often referred to as 'inspiration' or its absence as 'writers block'.

By looking at the different stages of life, it is evident that we are influenced by cognition and intuition. In order to live a meaningful life, the things we need are provided to us from a source. In our mind, thoughts are formed in an order on their own and because of that order, we lead an orderly life. From early childhood to late years the experiences our consciousness gathers and the awareness of its organized and powerful use is also provided by that source.

This internal working can be seen in the different types of personalities and interests. Consciousness gets its signal of centrality and aptitude from the unconscious. For instance, two children of same parents usually have different aptitudes and abilities. Even though socially they belong to the same economic strata and receive equal attention from the parents. They go to the same school but with age their conscious interests become different. One takes interest in arts while the other aspires to become a lawyer. One excels in academics and gets good grades while the other does not. We would not be able to find any clues if we were going to look into the outward circumstances. Similarly, if these children were asked why they take certain interest in one subject but not the other, they would not be able to answer that as well. The truth is that the impressed mark of the unconscious determines the course of interest for the consciousness and the individual's ability, interest, and performance gets distinguished.

This can also be seen in the Animal Kingdom. In the lower animals as well as among insects there exists an individualized as well as collective cohesive consciousness. Moreover, we know that in the workings of that consciousness, cognition, or education plays no part. For example the making of the spider's web or the ability to fly among birds or the ability of honey-bee to make honey from the flowers are all the behavior we usually call innate behavior. None of these skills is taught in any way. What we are trying to point out is that behind the mechanism of the consciousness, there is a source. The consciousness is influenced by that source. Human life in all its different stages is influenced by that same source, but since we are so used to our daily routine, we hardly pay any attention to it. However, there are different aspects, which could not be termed as routine or ordinary. Therefore based on experiences and observations human cognition is forced to classify these into different layers. Psychology talks about subconsciousness and unconsciousness while Parapsychology deals with the sixth sense, inner voice, or Extra Sensory Perception (ESP). Religious figures introduce us to conscience, intuition and the spirit. Hence, all branches of knowledge recognize the existence of a source or entity besides the brain. More interestingly, even non-religious people (e.g., Karl Marx) are forced to recognize a unit, which is beyond the scope of human intelligence or consciousness... Nature.

In other words, there are two brains in humans. One of them is the outward one while the other is hidden. The more this outward brain is connected to the hidden brain the more peaceful a life we lead. Our angle of perception gets wider and the capability of the brain to receive and comprehend the intuitive information it receives from the hidden brain is enhanced. All Spiritual branches of knowledge (including Sufism) are based on the notion that a person be able to use the spiritual brain as much as possible. The transferring of thoughts without material medium (Telepathy); receiving information without the help of any material medium (*kashaf*); making changes in things and thoughts with the spiritual power (*tasarraf*); knowledge of spiritual formulas; visiting other worlds; observing angels and *jinns*, Heaven, Hell, the Divine Throne and glimpses of the Divine Attributes, all these are possible only when the spiritual brain of the individual is activated and functional.

4
Waves of Thought

In the human mind the waves of information from the cosmos convert into thoughts. Just as when you throw a stone on a still pond of water, it creates circular waves in the pond; in the same manner, waves of thoughts are created when cosmic information energy enters our mind.

When we look into our daily routine, it becomes obvious that right away when we wake up, thoughts of work or school bumps into our mind. Being under the influence of those thoughts, we start our day by dressing and then set out for work or school. On our way to work, we see hundreds and thousands of images right before our eyes. At the same time, we hear different voices (or noises).There are certain images that draw our attention, such as a car wreck on a freeway that leaves a lasting impression in our mind. Likewise, we cannot help but read whatever is written on the new billboard, but once we arrive at work or school, our job or schoolwork draws our attention.

After a day at school or work when we return to our homes, domestic issues engulf our mind. After finishing some chores we then turn to either entertainment, like watching TV or listening to music or go out for dinner or movies or hang out with our friends and buddies until it gets late and then we finally go to our bed. The next day is spent more or less in the same way.

If we take any given period of the day, we realize that our attention never stays on any given matter for very long. It shifts along with the incoming thoughts. Troublesome thoughts worry us and we could not help but worry endlessly about it. On the other hand, any happy thought sets our mind into the emotional bliss of happiness. Similarly, thoughts of any past unpleasant incident set our mind into looking into the fine details of that incident.

By examining our daily routine of mental occupation, it is evident that our mind is constantly engrossed in the affairs of the surrounding environment and the normal waking period of the day is routinely consumed by the mental hustle and bustle. We are constantly bombarded by the incoming thoughts related to the surroundings and hardly any time is spent when our focus is shifted from the seemingly never-ending thoughts. This throng of thoughts becomes a hurdle for consciousness and because of that it never pays any attention to the esoteric life. Just as it is harder to inside the pond when the waves are on top of it, the mind is therefore, unable to see the inner reflections.

Reflections that falls on the mind are either light or strong based on their impressions. Strong impressions can be perceived by the consciousness, however lighter impressions on the mind are beyond the approach of the consciousness. Hence, very light reflections become oblivious. As long as the mental focus remains on the inside waves of thoughts, peeping inside the mind remains unattainable. But when the focus is diverted from the thoughts that are surfacing, then the mental vision starts functioning in the inner realm, and the lighter reflections can now be seen that otherwise are ignored or unseen.

The central idea of the above explanation is that in order to acquire spiritual knowledge and to awaken the paranormal abilities, the most fundamental thing to have is mental concentration. The first and foremost lesson that is taught or learned in the science of spiritual awakening is the state of emptiness of mind. Mental emptiness is the first lesson of the spiritual science. Through this ability, the student is able to observe the spiritual realm free from any worldly thoughts.

This does not mean, however, that no thought at all would come into the mind. Mental emptiness is a state in which concentration is focused on a single idea or point in such a way that the person would not let any other thought in his or her mind at will. It could also be defined as the mind being so deeply focused on a single idea or thought that all other thoughts simply become less important and eventually disappear. You would encounter difficulties in practicing 'mental emptiness' in the beginning. The reason is that we are not used to this condition. However, by continued practice it is attainable. The descriptive term for the mental emptiness is Muraqaba (or meditation). Mental emptiness is evident in many aspects of our daily life.

Example

When we sit down to write an essay or a story, we grab the pen or the keyboard to write. The mind then starts the process of choosing words and so on. The environment in which we perform these tasks may have various things or sounds that normally distract our attention. Nevertheless, we are not distracted and remained focused on writing the material. Our thoughts and actions revolve around the same points.

The same goes for driving. While driving a vehicle, our entire focus remains on the traffic as well as the mechanical aspect of driving. Moreover, because of that mental focus our body is able to control and operate the vehicle. During driving we try our best to remain focused on the road and the incoming traffic; while at the same time we chat with the passengers in the vehicle, listen to our favorite radio or music and various thoughts cross our minds, but our intentional focus never shifts from driving.

More or less the same state of mind is needed for performing Muraqaba. For 10-15 minutes or an hour the person who is meditating tries to remain focused or concentrated on a single idea or thought, while at the same time mentally disengaged from all other activities or thoughts. In other words, Muraqaba in essence is to become thoughtless in a thought.

During the Muraqaba, all of those resources are applied through which the mind disengages from external influences and becomes absorbed in a single thought or idea. When the influx of thoughts of outward environment is suspended, then the latent source of information starts to surface through which the person envisions, listens, touches and performs all other functions that are commonly known as the paranormal or spiritual abilities.

Rumi has explained the same phenomenon in his verse.

> *Eyes are shut*
> *so are ears*
> *and lips are sealed*
> *yet sight still beholds.*

5
Third Eye

Under physical or conscious senses we see through the physical eye. When our eyes are closed, then the information that comes to us through normal vision gets suspended and we are unable to see anything. This is simply how the mechanism of the physical eye works.

It is often stated that we see through our eyes but if we had paid attention, we would have come to realize that eyes are not the only thing needed for vision. If the system that transports the information from the sight screen to the brain were suspended then the person would be unable to see even with perfect eyes. This suggests that eyes are only a part in the mechanism of vision. They are *not* everything.

Occasionally, we observe someone sleeping with his/her eyes open. In that instance, the person is unaware of what is going on in his/her surrounding. Eyes and the nervous system that supports sight is all there but he is unable to see. That proves that the brain has to be in an attentive state for us to see.

Example

Every day we leave home to go to work (or school) and almost daily, we see various things on our way to work. Yet if someone asks us to list everything that we saw, we would only be able to list those that we paid attention to. Another similar example would be when we find ourselves in the midst of a deep thought and the voices or things that are happening in our surroundings do not cross our mind.

The human mind has a continuous flow of thoughts and imagination. By looking deeper we find that all the activities and colorfulness of life are related to those thoughts and imaginations. All natural and innate urges emerge from thoughts as well, not only mundane activities of life but arts and science begin with human imagination.

When we look externally, the information from the surrounding environment serves as the axis for the thoughts. However often someone who is sitting, being unaware of the surroundings, is able to receive the flow of thoughts and visual images in the screen of his mind. This suggests that when the reflection of the outward falls on the screen of sight through light, then the physical eye sees the outward images.

However, when thoughts and imaginations emerge on the mental screen then the light of the outward plays no part in it. We feel the reflection of the imagination in the same way as we do for the reflection of the outward image. The reflection of the imagination may be dim though it contains the same meaning as the image of the outward. Hence, we can say that the process of vision occurred in both instances.

Often we experience an event that has left us with lasting impressions or a personality with whom we are emotionally attached so that when the mind goes to any of the above and the focus deepens as well, then the minute details of the event or the image of that person emerges on the screen of the mind. That image emerges in such a manner that we feel it like a pictorial form. No image comes from the outward. Nevertheless, we feel that pictorial image right in front of us, as if the image were in front of our eyes.

In the same way when we are asleep, our eyes are closed and yet we behold different scenes in the dream. It has happened in our experience that sometimes when we see an event-taking place in a dream or semi-drowsiness, a few days later the same event actually takes place.

The above examples from daily life illustrate the fact that in seeing those images or feeling the reflection of those images the involvement of our physical eye is absolutely nothing. What we are trying to explain is that human vision is independent of any material elements for its true functioning. In one manner, it works through the means of physical eye and in the other style or manner it is entirely free of any need of a physical eye. The style of vision that functions without the means of physical eye is often referred as inner vision, esoteric vision or simply as the third eye.

If we were to define man in terms of spiritual sciences it would simply be as vision. Vision is dependent on information. Information is constantly received in the mind and there it eventually turns into the vision.

Any information that comes from the outside is elucidated in the cleanest form by the sense of vision. The sense of vision is responsible for providing the mind with as much information as possible. When this sense works within the physical body, the physical eye does the "observation ". However, the same sense can function without the means of a physical eye. When the movement of the physical eye is suspended but the sight is focused on any given object then the flow of information stops. The sense of sight or vision then starts ascending.

Unless the sense of sight performs its entire function, its role remains incomplete. Under the Laws of Creation, it is bound to perform its given function. When the sense of sight ascends, man starts to see with eyes closed the hidden realm. At that moment, the vision observes all the different dimensions of the entire Universe. Those are the forms and figures that a step later manifest as material forms. These figures are called the esoteric or spiritual world. Consistency in Muraqaba forces the sense of vision to hide behind the physical world and turn the focus of the vision toward the world, which could not be seen with the physical eyes.

When we see from our eyes, eyelids move and the process of winking happens. Continuously doing so puts a pressure on eyeballs. They move in different directions because of it. Through these movements of eyeballs, the sense of outward light works inside the brain. In addition, the brain gets the information as to what and where everything lies in the environment. All these movements happen when a person is focused on the outward world and wants to get as much information as possible. Involvement in the outward world evolves into specific movements of the nerves. Eyeballs move and through winking create movement in the nerves. Movements similar to these are essential for the working of physical vision and due to them, the mechanism of 'limited vision' works.

If we focus the sight into a point or a *circle (chakra)* and suspend the process of blinking then this would result in higher concentration and the feelings of the existing environment are lowered. Another aspect of this experiment is that *circle (chakra)* gradually disappears and a new screen takes it place. The reason for that is by not doing the blinking the eyeballs get distress and when only one scene stays on the screen of the consciousness then this condition rises.

When the mind is under the influence of material (physical) senses, it goes from one thought to another constantly and does not stay on any one thought for long. However, when things happen the other way round, the physical senses become inactive or dormant. This happens when on the screen of the mind, only one image stays and blinking is suspended. This gazing creates a bumper in the flow of waves, which works in the consciousness. When blinking stops, the physical vision becomes inactive. When this suspension stays past its limits, the angle of vision or sight alters and inner vision or sight comes into motion. When a person does Muraqaba, all those factors come into motion that activates the inner sight (vision) by suspending the outward vision.

Both outward and inward information depends on light. Just as light is the source of information for the outward it is also the source for the inner information. When the form of light changes so does the perception of the vision and the feelings. Just as when the Sun rises, everything in the environment lit because of it and the way we feel is evidently different during the day than during the dark hours of the night. When blue colored sunglasses are worn, everything seems bluish; when it is a red color lens then all we see seems reddish. Working continuously under intense high voltage lights would make the nerves feel weak and fatigued but when the environment contains natural colors or scenery, the nerves then get soothing effects. When we look through binoculars, distant objects come closer and when a microscope is used then even the unseen objects become visible. Inside the circle of the physical (material) world, there are numerous objects which our eyes could not see. Minute particles, atom, electrons, protons, and other atomic particles remain out of our sight. The longer the distance the more we are unable to see the attributes or the details of objects. We could not even see the trees and its leaves. Due to the visionary limitations, buildings and their features appear to be misty and hazy.

According to Physics, in an atom, electrons revolve around the nucleus within the boundaries of its orbit. In a liquid, molecules move freely in all directions. Inside the gases, their movements exceed even further. There are various things that we could not see but they are known to us because of their qualities or effects, such as electrical flow, magnetic field, x-rays, and other various forms of rays.

When we look into any invention with the help of formulas of Physics, many minute details and hidden angles come to the surface. When we see through the lenses of a microscope, even the smallest bacteria, viruses and other tiny particles become visible. With the help of an electron microscope even the "ghost" of an electron is visible. With a telescope, distant objects can be seen as near. The type and strength of the lenses determine what could be visible to the eye.

This is the story of the light that works in the outward world. When the angle of the outward light is altered, our vision changes with it. In the same manner the inner information that comes into the mind is also dependent on the workings of light. By closing the eyes, the mind is being focused and the flow of outward light is stopped. Then inward light takes it place by infusing into the senses.

6

Film and Screen

Our mind is a screen on which the movie of life is being displayed. The screen consists of two layers. On one of its layers the movie of physical senses is displayed. Any wishes and needs that enter the mind in the form of thought fall on the outer layer of the conscious mind, and through those needs, the different systems of the physical body work. The second layer of the screen exists in the depths of the mind. It can also be called the inner layer. At this layer, the photographic reflection of the information is displayed in the form of light. Under normal condition, this screen does not come in front of our eyes.

Example

In the movie theater, the movie projector is placed on the opposite side, facing the screen. Once the film is loaded inside the projector, it is turned on with the light switch. As the film rolls, the images in the film fall on the screen with the help of the light in which they travel. Those images on the screen become 'alive' right where they strike it. However, when we look at the space between the projector and the screen all we see is a stream of light coming out of the area where projector is working. Those rays of light carry all the images visible on the screen. Hence, this process could be divided into three parts. First, the images of the film; second, the light on which those images travel and eventually fall on the screen; and third, the screen itself on which those images are displayed. When physical senses move inside us then we see the film on our physical screen.

When we are under the influence of physical senses then we see the film on our physical screen. At that moment, the reflection of the film falls on the outer surface (layer) of consciousness. Innately our memory makes us dependent on gravity. We, under the restrictions of time and space, can only observe the 'present moment'.

Our mind also carries a screen of light in which the cosmic film is displayed. On that screen, we can even see those objects that are otherwise hidden from our physical eye. Under this method of observation, the restriction of time and space plays no part. In the present moment, we can see any moment, whether it is past or future, near or far.

Whatever that we see is traveling on those factors that are apparently invisible to our eyes. Nevertheless, without their presence, no action can manifest. Every action of the existing being is inter-linked with one another and creation of every moment depends on the previous one. The first moment leads to the second one and the second one leads to the third. We simply cannot but recognize the existence of the activities in life, which we refer as 'past' and those which are called 'future,' in the 'present' moment.

All the attributes and information of life are attached to the physical being. Our eyes could not normally see them. However, whenever we need them they come forward. Physical (outward) senses are unable to see them, but we simply cannot deny their existence. The level of this attribute exists in its proper form in the realm of lights (Non-physical world). This system acts through waves or through the chemical properties of the cell.

When we see someone, for example John Doe, our eyes could only see the body made out of flesh and bones. The personal attributes of John Doe remain hidden from our sight. For example, whether John Doe is kind hearted, well-behaved, is or is not sensitive and so on. His brain contains unlimited information of scientific knowledge. His memory has registered millions of images. There are numerous activities going on inside John's body and mind which remain hidden.

His life is a collection of various activities from the time of his birth to the present. Every mental and physical activity is a motion. John's whole life is like a movie in which every action (motion) is an image. However, even a single image can never be removed from the life of John Doe. The man that exists before our very eyes only as a statue of bones and flesh but his past, his future, and all of his abilities and attributes are hidden from the eyes. That means that real John Doe is the name of the attributes and the body is merely an outward display of those attributes.

The hidden life of John Doe and all of his qualities exist in the form of a film or record. The material manifestation of this film is his physical being itself, which could also be called consciousness. Our eyes could only see the John Doe of limited qualities. However, the unlimited qualities and attributes remain hidden from our sight. Nevertheless, no one can deny the existence of those qualities.

The hidden record or the film always coexists with the mind. For example, when we see someone whom we had not seen in twenty five years then we do not have to memorize the events of the past twenty five years nor do we physically enter the time zone of twenty five years ago, instead we instantly recognize that person. This means that the subconscious has the record of those twenty five years. When the record came into motion then the interim period simply is deleted in order to bring back the twenty five year-old personality. And our mind was able to see that 'moment' which exists in the record in which the twenty five year-old personality is stored.

The seed of any tree is considered to be the earliest form of its existence. This same seed, when conjoined with soil and water and under a specific temperature, comes into motion. It seems illogical to believe that tiny seed holds all the information regarding the whole life of that tree, its branches, leaves, fruits and its future generation. Nevertheless, it is an undeniable truth. As this seeds grows, it completes various stages of growth. In other words, the physical being of the tree (i.e. seed) holds the entire record of its life. The same record through stages and fixed term manifests as a whole tree.

According to Sufism all the records of attributes exist at a level that is called the world of lights (luminous world). This record could be accessed in the form of watching a film. The basic element of watching the 'inner movie' is to move the sight (or vision) away from the physical screen. In this practice all those methods are used upon which the sight shifts its interest from watching the outer screen to the inner screen. During this attempt, the consciousness become subdued and the sight rejects that screen that usually comes in front of the vision during the conscious state of mind. Through consistent practice, the focus of the sight shifts to the screen which exists in the inner layer of the mind and on which the film or movie of the hidden reality of the universe is displayed.

To focus our sight on the inner film is definitely not a part of our daily routine. Hence our lower-self tries to end that quest. Different thoughts cross our mind and we tend to get bored with it. In order to keep our focus on the inner screen we have to repeat the process often to get used to it.

The 'Point of Essence' (*nuqta dhat*) that lies inside the Man, can observe the wonders of the Universe on both screens. The reason why we are unaware of the inner screen is that all of our interests lie with the outer screen. We simply do not get interested in watching the inner screen.

7
Motions of the Spirit

Life that is known to us as material life is entirely composed of physical actions and functions. For example when we are thirsty or hungry, we immediately prepare or assemble food and drink that ultimately becomes part of our body. In the same way, job exploration, happiness, and sadness are all functions based on physical actions. However, if look deeply we would see that everything is being guided by our intelligence. All these physical actions with their every detail first descend into the mind. From there the 'physical' machine simply obeys its command. As when we are thirsty, the need to squelch the thirst emerges first in the mind. Then based on the knowledge we have in our brain that deals with extinguishing the thirst, we put our will into it. When the knowledge of thirst and all its details runs into motion with all of its energy then our brain sends the command to the physical part to deal with that need. Because of it, the body comes into motion by drinking water and hence completing the need of it.

Example

When someone puts his mind into writing an essay or story, the first thing that happens is that the draft of the essay and all its details appear in his mind. Then the writer pens the entire detailed draft on paper. That detailed draft is called the essay, story, or novel and so on.

Whether it is a need to quench the thirst or write an essay, what first comes into our mind is the detailed picture. The function of the 'human machine' is simply to convert that picture into physical action. In other words, unless any action is first created and organized in the mind, physical response does not occur.

The working of physical actions is called the material world while what is beyond the physical actions is referred to as the spiritual world. In the spiritual world all the feelings and all dimensions exist in the form of Divine Knowledge. The example of the process of thirst was given earlier. When the need of thirst and the will to drink occurs in the mind, then the person feels the entire process in the dimensions of the knowledge. However, these motions do not translate into the physical action. They only manifest in one point; after that the physical action takes place.

The bottom line of this detailed account is that actions of the human mind appear in two circles. In the first circle information works without physical action, in the second they work along with the motion. When physical action occurs all laws of gravity come into motion. Moments are subject to chronological order. One moment evolves into the second and third subsequent moments. Unless the second moment occurs, the third could not. On the contrary, under the other circle the actions, human soul, or ego are free from the physical body. At that point, the human ego frees itself from the clutches of moments of chronological order.

Example

The mind sends a message that in order to get physical energy food is needed. When we follow up on this information we have to go through different stages in chronological order before we accomplished our objective. First, we have to cultivate wheat, then we processed it to make it flour. Then we convert into dough to first bake then finally to eat it. This is how a physical brain functions. On the contrary, when spiritual brain is in motion and we need anything to eat then we do not have to go through those steps. The moment the need for bread comes in the spiritual mind, the bread manifests itself.

The clearest example of this in the physical life is dreaming. When we wake up in the morning, the senses immediately get busy trying to connect with the environment. Moreover, as long as we are awake our nervous system controls our every movement throughout the day. However, when we fall asleep, the human motions take a back seat but the active role of ego does not stop here. During dreaming, even though the body remains in a somewhat comatose state, all the motions and sounds are registered by the mind almost the same way; we see and hear those things in this awake stage. The only difference is that the boundaries of time and space no longer exist during dreaming and feeling and sensation draws to a single point. For example, in a dream we see our friend who may live very far away but when we are engaged in a conversation with him we do not feel there was any space separating us.

Similarly, we go to bed at midnight, and during dreaming, we go from one country to the other. We see a film or chain of events. However, if we were awakened by accident and see the time it probably would be just few minutes past our sleeping time. If those chains of events and movements happened with our physical body then it would have needed weeks, months and hundred of hours plus thousands of miles of travel.

One of the qualities of the soul (*nafas*) that remain active during wakefulness and sleep is memory. Man uses this power throughout his life but hardly realizes that when a period of childhood is recalled, in one moment he is able to access the entire memory of his childhood. Even though decades may have passed since then and he may have gone through thousands of changes when the mind travels into the past, then in the one thousandth part of second it reaches the period of childhood. We not only feel the events of the past but these events are displayed in such a way as if someone were watching a movie.

Oftentimes the difference of feelings becomes so deep that the consciousness is able to perceive it. While doing some work if our concentration increases enormously and conscious sighting centers on a single point then this could become an experimental observation.

Example

While reading an interesting book our concentration intensifies to such an extent that it negates time. Often when we are done with reading, it seems like only a few minutes have passed, but only after looking at our watch do we realize that a lot of time has passed. In the same manner while waiting for someone, a few minutes feels like hours.

In this era of Freudian Psychology a dream is simply regarded as stored-up thoughts of memory and irrational imagination. However, the real life experiences of dreams prove otherwise. Ever since history has been recorded, in every geographical area and at all times the importance of dreams has been recognized. In the history of the science of the soul and in religious matters as well dreams have a prominent position. People from all economic and educational levels have experienced this phenomenon. Even though every one of us sees something every night in our sleep often we see something that even after awakening its effect is not forgotten. Some dreams are so deep that their effects are simply transformed into awakening right after that person wakes up. Some people have felt the taste of things that they ate during the dream long after being woken up and it feels almost like the taste of things that we eat during our waking hours. Erotic dreams result in the same kind of pleasure and ejaculatory discharge as during actual sexual intercourse. Often an event or incident that was seen in a dream happens within days or months, exactly the way it was shown during that dream. That points out that just as we can replay the events of the past (flashbacks), in the same manner we can also read the signs of future events. In the *Qur'an* (Koran) and other holy sculptures the dream is often referred to as a vision (*roya*). In these scriptures, it is mentioned that the dream is an agency through which man can access the realms of the unseen and the ability to dream (vision) provides the man, the knowledge of the unseen or paranormal in his normal physical level of existence.

The prophet Joseph saw in his dream that the Sun, moon and eleven stars prostrating before him which suggested that in due future he will be given the gift of prophecy and Divine Knowledge (*ilm ladani*). Years later in prison, he interpreted the dreams of his fellow inmates, the royal cook and the bartender, and correctly predicted their future. When the king saw a dream, Prophet Joseph predicted that there would be a famine followed by surplus of grains. All of which came true the way Prophet Joseph had predicted it. Notable to mention is the fact that among these dreams that we just discussed one of them is of a Prophet, however the other three are of ordinary folks. All of these dreams were carrying news of the future.

The human soul or ego remains constantly in motion. Just as the awakened time is usually spent in one moment or the other, similarly a dream is also a motion. We are always aware of our actions while we are awake, which is why all of our interests lie with the awakened state of mind. Nevertheless, not all of the events of the awakened period register in our memory. Only those events are stored that leave a lasting impression on our consciousness for whatever reason.

Example

When we are traveling from one city to another, there are places that we like and others that do not feel pleasant. We see numerous billboards, and cars go by right in front of our eyes. In some places, we see tall trees and fertile land. However, when we arrive at the other city and if asked to mention everything that we saw, it would not be easy for us to describe everything that we observed during our journey. We may be able to give a few details such as where we stayed or maybe an event that we saw, but for the rest of the journey we would simply declare that we did not pay much attention to it. In other words, when we are focused on something, it is registered in our memory, while of no interest went unnoticed.

The same rule applies to dreams. During dreaming, the physical senses remain dormant but the spirit goes through different actions and feelings and our mind only comprehends those events in which it maintains an interest. That is why we can only relate those parts of dreams on which our focus was kept and the events on which we do not focus are not connected by our own consciousness.

Sometimes consciousness sees the actions of the soul in an organized fashion and the motions of soul so fuse right into the mind that getting the meaning out of it is hardly difficult. Those dreams are called the "true dreams." When this state progresses it reaches the level of inspiration(*ilhaam*) and revelations (*kashaf*).

Nature has enforced its law on all creatures including humans: that they could not break away from the sense of dream (nocturnal consciousness). In order to keep the physical side of human life it is imperative to enter the senses of dream. That is why every individual, however reluctantly, is bound to get sleep. In addition, when he comes out of sleep into the physical world, he finds himself with renewed energy for the fulfillment of his physical action (or life). Nocturnal senses are such a unique gift of Nature that every one has it. We can benefit from it even further if we so desire.

Spiritual science begins with this basic lesson: we are not just a body of flesh and bones. Along with the body there is an agency attached to it known as spirit (*ruh*), which is really its essence. The human spirit is able to move without the body and if we can rise to a certain level, we can go on a spiritual journey without our body.

This movement of the spirit occurs unconsciously every day during dreaming. There always comes a period during the day or night when we feel a certain pressure; unintentionally sense becomes heavier. Eyelids feel the load as well and we start getting groggy. Owing to this biological pressure, we ultimately surrender ourselves to sleep. Eyelids get shut and our senses want to get away from the surrounding environment. Consciousness rejects every thought that could interfere with sleep. In a short while nerves get quiet and we move from the state of drowsiness to light sleep and then into deep sleep.

This change of state of senses occurs without our intentional efforts. We unintentionally and sometimes unwillingly move into the nocturnal senses. That is why whatever we see in a dream, some of that remains in our memory while other things do not. When we enter this dream state in a way that our consciousness remains active and awake then the flight of spirit becomes an observational experiment and we are able to remember it.

The easiest way to achieve this is to enter intentionally the dream state without going to sleep. In other words, the same procedure that brings us from an awakened state into the nocturnal one unintentionally could be used to bring us to the nocturnal state at will without ever going into actual sleep.

If we have to define Muraqaba with respect to dreams and the awakened state then we can say that the Muraqaba is the journey into the dream world while being fully awake. In other words, Muraqaba is a process through which we try to enter the nocturnal state but our consciousness remains alert. During Muraqaba, all those conditions are created that a person goes through during the transformation between senses. After closing the eyes, breathing slows as well. The physical body relaxes so that we may not feel the its presence during Muraqaba. Mentally we free ourselves from all thoughts and worries and focus on one single idea (or imagination).

When we see someone who is engaged in Muraqaba, it seems like someone is sleeping while sitting with their eyes closed. However, in reality, his consciousness is not dormant the way it is during sleep. Hence, during Muraqaba we enter into a state (condition) that is dominant during dreaming. The moment conscious senses enter stillness the diurnal senses are enveloped by the nocturnal senses. During this state we can use all those abilities and forces that work during dreaming. Past and future, near and far become meaningless. We become free of all the limitations of the physical body.

This ability increases to a level where the nocturnal and diurnal senses become parallel and human consciousness becomes aware of the affairs of nocturnal actions just the way it is aware of the diurnal actions. Hence under nocturnal senses, we can use our own spirit (*ruh*) to carry out our wishes.

8
Electrical System

When we contemplate matter then material laws (Physics) and material attributes come to the surface. However, when our mind goes deeply into the matter then we become aware of the world which is the basis of matter. We can call that the world of light. When scientists research the ingredients of matter, the atom and its particles come into light. Among the atomic particles, electrons have dual attributes. On one hand, it is a material particle, on the other it is merely a ray. The system of rays inside the atom points to the world of illumination or light. Hence whatever we see in our environment on one hand has a physical side and on the other, it is a halo of light. Whatever motion takes place in that halo of light reflects physical being. Based on a scientific principle, if a number of electrons and protons are altered then that atom changes its form. In a nuclear reaction, uranium after fusion converts to plutonium. Hence, those atomic particles that belong to the world of rays, if any changes occur to them then they change their shape. When a change takes place in the world of rays or light (non-physical world) then the same change is reflected in the physical identity of that element.

Just as with every physical being, a system of electrical flow works in the same way, since humans also possess the electrical system. According of Sufism, Man is not just a statue of flesh and bones; besides being a physical being, he is also a luminary being. Moreover, that luminary being is its essence. That being is the electrical ray or current.

Generators (*latifa*)

Three generators work inside the human body. These generators produce three different types of electrical currents. The combination of these three current is in fact a man.

Example

The light of a candle is composed of three parts.

One: Color of fire.
Two: Light of fire.
Three: Heat that is produced because of that burning.

When we describe a candle it is usually meant the combination of the above three states. No single attribute can be separated from its existence. Just like the candle, human senses are also subject to three electrical rays. All thoughts, imaginations, and feelings, whether they are outward or inward, obvious or latent, are made of various mixtures of electrical current.

All three generators are controlled by a central power station referred to as Divine Will (*amr*), Spirit (*ruh*), or the Divine Light (*tadjalli*).

The electric charge that is produced by generator no.1 is exceptionally delicate and carries high speed. Its strength or potential is extremely strong. Due to its high speed it keeps the mind linked to all the dimensions of the Universe. Also because of its high speed, its reflection that falls on the screen of the human mind is very dim. That reflection is called the whim (*wahma*). All feelings and knowledge begin with it. It is the most delicate form of thought that can only be felt in the depth of perception. When it deepens, it becomes a thought.

The electric charge that is created by generator no.1 is composed of two parts. One has more strength then the other. The same electric flow first gains speed and then slow down. The more powerful and high-speed charge is the consciousness of the Universe and the weaker one is what we call a whim.

Generator no.2 also creates two types of current, one of which is positive and the other negative. When the negative wave enters whim, it is converted into a thought. Actually, thought is the detailed picture of whim. However, it is hidden from the sight as well. When the positive current envelops the thought it turns it into imagination. When thought gains some form and figure it is referred as imagination. Imagination is such a figure, which remains latent from the sight but the mind figures out its picture and other details.

The purpose of the electric current of generator no.3 is give depth to feelings. This electric charge acts in the form of waves. This means that one of its motions is ascending and the other descending. In other words, these two movements give two types of feelings to the mind. Ascending movement is the colorfulness of feelings. In this movement, the imagination becomes so strong that you are involuntarily drawn toward action. Descending movement is the action or its display.

The Divine Will (*amr*) or Divine Light (*tadjalli*) carries the entire knowledge or science in the form of a record. When this record is activated, it turns into a whim. This action is called the current no.1.

The negative wave of current no.2 gives whim the forms and figure of a thought. Through thought, all creatures are connected in one chain. That is why all creatures share the basic needs, for example, hunger, thirst, anger; need to reproduce and so on.

The positive flow of current no.2 gives you the awareness of the imaginations of your own kind (species).

The descending flow of current no.3 solidifies the perception while ascending flow brings colorfulness to it. During ascending flow, all your feelings after disconnecting themselves from the body emancipate from time and space. Descending flow manifest through eyes, ears, nose and limbs. Ascending manifests through faculties of vision, hearing, speaking and touch functions without any physical organs.

All three currents pass through the mind and it moves in all three states. However, according to whichever current has the strong reflection on the screen of mind, you find yourself moving in the attributes of that current. If current no.3 is subdued by the sensation of current no.2 or 1 then you move with the speed of imagination, thought and whim and all hidden information are received in the form of a film.

By practicing Muraqaba the strength of current 2 and 3 gradually increases. By increasing the strength we mean that the receiver of the brain is able to receive this information in a better way.

3 currents:

As we have mentioned earlier there are three different types of electrical current that work inside the human body. These three currents are the three forms of perception. Each possesses complete identity. Each current creates a separate body of a man. Hence man has three being in him. In other words he has three bodies: a physical body, a luminous body and a body made of pure light (*nur*). These three bodies function simultaneously though physical body (consciousness) is only aware of the physical actions. For example, numerous body functions are performed inside the physical body. Lungs perform the respiratory functions; the liver does its own work and inside the brain a spectacular phenomenon occurs through electrical current. Through cell division, old cells convert into new cells. Most of these functions are neither provided by consciousness nor does our conscious mind control it. Without conscious knowledge, these functions are performed automatically. Luminous and pure light bodies also work inside us but our consciousness is unable to feel them. Only during dream and Muraqaba (meditation) do we get an awareness of the luminous body. During this condition, our physical body remains inactive. In spite of that, we perform all our functions of life.

During this condition the luminous body is able to move. This body is also known as Aura or the *jism mithali*. When the power of thought is increased, the actions of the aura become evident and we can use it at our will. The speed of the aura is sixty thousands times greater then the physical body. During dreaming, the body of pure light (*nur*) also becomes functional but its speed is so fast that we are unable to remember its actions. The body of pure light travels a thousand times faster than the aura. If the strength of thought is increased to its desired level then you could become aware of the body of pure light as well.

Spiritual beings travel with their luminous and pure light bodies by achieving perfection in Muraqaba. Through Muraqaba, the conscious state of humans is dissolved into the luminous body. You then become aware of all the information that is already loaded in the luminous body. Here we would like to clarify that this light is not the light we see with our naked eyes. Instead this light is unseen by our physical eye. Moreover, when conscious state dissolves into the pure light realm, the pure-light body becomes functional. At that moment, you, through these pure light waves, will be able to cross the boundaries of time and space.

9

Three Layers

E very human being is composed of three bodies or Spirits. Each body is then comprised of two subtle substances (*latifa*, plural *lata'if*).

al-nafs al-ammara: **a.k.a.** Animal Soul, lower Self, *ruh hevani* = Soul(*nafs*)+ Heart(*qalb*).

al-nafs al-lawwama: **a.k.a.** Human Soul, Ego, *ruh insani*= Spirit (*ruh*) + Consciousness (*sirr*).

al-nafs al- mutma'inna **a.k.a.** Contented Soul, Higher Self, *ruh azam* = Mystery (*khafi*)+Arcanum(*akhfa*).

These six subtle substances (or *chakra*, which we are going to call spheres) are further divided into six more layers of light and pure light (*nur*). From the three waves of light, diurnal senses are formed while through three pure-light (*nur*) waves nocturnal senses are formed. The layers of light are necessary for the diurnal senses while the pure-light waves are needed for the functioning of the nocturnal life.

Every one of us wakes up after sleeping. After waking up when our eyes first open, we enter into the conscious senses. We can call this state as semi-awakening. What we mean by semi-awakening is that during this stage we are not yet fully entered into consciousness. However, the moment we wake up from sleeping and enter the first state of awakening, our soul is inundated by thoughts and actions; meaning that the awakened styles of thoughts and actions start flowing collectively.

After semi-awakening the second stage starts. During this stage, our mental alertness deepens. As it deepens the drowsiness that our brain feels, ends. During this stage, we enter into the state of exhilaration or slight intoxication (*khumaar*). This feeling of slight intoxication goes up and down and it activates the sphere of Heart (*qalb*). When the feeling of exhilaration gets stronger, it turns into *vijdan* (Intuitive ecstasy). This is the third stage of wakefulness. During this ecstasy the sphere of Spirit (*ruh*) is activated.

First stage:
Semi wakefulness (initiation of conscious senses) = Thoughts and action converage into one point = sphere of Soul activates.

Second stage:
The drowsiness decreases, gives away to alertness = exhilaration = sphere of Heart activates.

Third stage:
Exhilaration gets deeper = ecstasy = sphere of Spirit activates.

Just as there are three stages of wakefulness, there are three stages of sleep as well. The way we enter into wakefulness by going through three stages, we enter into sleep by going through three stages as well. The stage between sleep and wakefulness is *ghanood* (drowsiness).

During drowsiness the sphere of *sirr* (conscience) is activated. The second stage of sleep, which could be labeled as light sleep, is the movement of the sphere of *khafi* (mystery). The third and final stage of sleep, which is often called 'deep sleep', is the movement of the *akhfa* (arcanum) sphere.

A point to ponder is that at the start of all these states we all go through the state of stillness. When we wake up our mind is usually at peace and is filled with a feeling of emptiness. Similarly, during other states as well, we go through this period of brief tranquility. This means to shift from one state to the other, serenity is essential. Just as during wakefulness every condition begins with that tranquility; in a same way, drowsiness senses also experience slight tranquility and after some moment this serenity of senses get deeper and turns into sleepiness. Early sleep after going through that quiet moment for a while turns into light sleep and then finally the quiet waves of deep sleep take over. That is why this influence is called deep sleep.

Laws of vision

Waking and dreaming are both related to senses. In one state, the speed of senses goes up while in the other it goes down. However, its condition does not change. Whether awake or sleeping the same kind and style of senses work. Waking or dreaming is actually two chambers of the brain or in other words, we have two brains. When senses are activated in one brain, it is called waking while when the senses are activated on the other, it is labeled as sleep. This means that the same kinds of senses are interchanging between waking and sleeping. This interchanging of senses is in fact life. When one kind of senses becomes dormant inside the brain, the other kind of senses simply takes over. During wakefulness the senses start working right when blinking starts that is the eyelids start hitting the eyeballs. When this process happens to us, we get out of sleep and enter the waking state. In our present time, we can use the example of a still camera as a metaphor. Even when there is film inside the camera and it has the lens as well, the camera is not going to work unless the button is pressed, causing the shutter to open and close within a tenth of a second or so.

In the same manner, unless the eyelids fall on the eyeballs (blinking) the frontal screen is not going to fall on the roll of the brain. This is the second stage of beholding during waking stage. The first stage begins when a thought enters the mind of the person as he wakes up after sleeping. That very thought becomes the barrier between sleep and awakening. As this thought deepens, the process of blinking starts and the scene in front of the eye begins transmitting to the screen of the brain.

The law of sight is that brain not only receives the picture of the outward image it also receives the information with it. By seeing, the mind puts meaning to that information. The image that falls on the screen of the mind through winking usually lasts for 15 seconds. Before those 15 seconds pass, the other images one by one fall on the screen and take over the previous image. That process remains consistent throughout waking period.

During the waking period the vision is directly linked to the eyeballs. Through blinking the eye camera actually takes the picture continuously. The rule is that if the blinking is suspended then the nerves inside the eye would stop working. The senses of the eye nerves work as long as the blinking process goes on. If the eyelids are forced to remain open and the movement of eyeball is stopped then the empty space comes in front of the vision and the picture-making process of the eyes would halt.

The entire Universe and all the creatures in this Universe are linked together in a cohesive manner. Different stages of life and the different times seem separated if seen from the outward eyes. However, the different stages of time and the various stages of life, no matter how different they may seem, are all linked to the center. Rays or waves serve as the communicator between the inhabitants of the Universe and the center. On the one hand, the waves from its central source descend and feed the individuals of the Universe and maintain centralization. On the other hand, after feeding the creatures of the Universe, these waves ascend back to their source. This never-ending process of ascent and descent *is* life. The distance that these waves cover ends up making this Universe look like a loop. With ascending and descending movements, this loop further divides into six more loops. The first circle of the Universe and the inhabitants of the Universe are called Soul (*nafs*). The

Soul is like a lamp from which the light is being emitted. The light or wave of this lamp is in fact vision or sight.

Evidently where there is a ray there will be a light and wherever light is, it brightens the environment. Wherever the lamp-light falls, it observes it. The light of the lamp is composed of many colors. The more colors it has the more colorfulness it brings to the environment. Intense light of the lamp goes from very low, bright to extremely bright. When low-intensity light falls on objects, whims about them enter our mind. Objects, on which medium-intensity light falls, create thoughts in our mind. When the high-intensity lights shine on objects their images form in our mind. Finally, when the extreme-intensity light falls on things, it can be seen by our sight. In fact, in order to see anything we go through these four stages.

In order to see and comprehend anything, first a whim about that thing enters the mind, meaning a very diminutive sketch is formed. When whim deepens, it becomes a thought. When a thought goes deep inside the mind, the picture of that object comes into being. When picture deepens then thought becomes imagination and when the picture in the imaginative way converts into form and figure than that object comes in range of our sight.

Cognition points out that to see is an ability that works even in the dimmest of light. Even the lightest of the sketch of any given thing, even if it is merely a whim, sends it to the vision, so that after going through the other three stages that object could be seen in the dimension of a form and figure with all its colorfulness.

The way we have described the rule of vision, all senses work in the same fashion. These senses are of smell, hearing, taste, and touch. All the interests and activities of life, events, actions, and entire system are based on the same above mentioned rule.

10
Heart of the Cosmos

We are continuously bombarded by different thoughts and images. It all happens without our will or intention. Moreover, without our discretion, thoughts gradually enter our consciousness. The thoughts, imaginations, feelings, and needs that are essential to human life consist of three stages.

One kind of thoughts and feelings lets human be aware of their own existence and to see themselves as human, which suggests that it is an individual feeling. This kind of consciousness exists in all creatures of this Universe. A goat is also aware of its existence and so is a pigeon.

The second consciousness lets the Self be aware of its own kind. For example, when this consciousness works inside a human being, humans beget other humans, just as from a cat spring other cats. The feelings of a human child are the same as its parents and the kitten has all those feelings that exist in a cat.

The collection of all these thoughts and awareness is a consciousness that exists in all creatures collectively, and the manifestation of that consciousness is "vision." This consciousness wherever it manifests, has a similar style. For example, a man sees water as water and so does a goat, which also drinks it to quench its thirst. The nature of this vision or consciousness has not changed from eternity to the modern day. Change of space also does not affect its role either.

Because of this consciousness all creatures are joined in an invisible bond. That is why the fundamentals of this Universe are the same. The forces of thirst, hunger, sadness, vision, hearing, and touch exist in all creatures. When these forces activate in species then each species applies that force in its own way. For example, hunger exists in both the lion and the goat. However, how they meet their needs is different. Each species' mind works on its own. In other words, the mind of that species becomes the individual consciousness of that individual.

The cosmic mind is like a seed of a tree. The stem of the tree, its branches, flower, fruits, everything has its foundation in that tiny seed. That one seed manifests itself in thousands of ways. If there were no seed then there would not be any tree. In the same fashion, all species and individuals of those species come into motion from the cosmic mind (consciousness). Species and all the thoughts, imaginations, and feelings that work in species are the extension of that one unit.

The analogy of an electrical power station can help us understand this even further. If for instance the mind of the species is considered as an electrical current and all the species as bulbs, then just as the electrical current goes to millions and trillions of electric bulbs from the power station; in the same manner the information from the cosmic mind (consciousness) reaches the species and its individuals. Since this information system works like the electrical system, the mind of all the species are interconnected with each other.

When we look into life itself, it becomes evident that one side of our mind functions in the physical life while the other side is the source of the information of life, in which all the information and actions are stored. That side influences our conscious life. In our physical body, numerous bodily functions are carried out without the conscious will or intention. For example in order to breathe, or to blink, or for the heart to beat, we do not need our will power. These functions are performed on their own in an orderly fashion.

During the reproductive process the features of species, its ideas, and information are transferred from the individual to their offspring. In reproduction, the role of individual consciousness is marginal; the main role is played by the species and cosmic consciousness.

With the advancement of genetics, it is not difficult to comprehend that the features of the newborn are always similar to that of his or her parents or relatives. The offspring always carry the features that belong to their own species. Not only does it inherit physical features but habits and behavior are transferred as well. In other words, the images of species and the attributes of cosmic consciousness are transferred like a record from parent to the child. Both of these records are stored in every newborn child. As the child grows, his consciousness broadens.

These facts point out that inside all of us there is an intelligent and authoritative system that works without will or intention. In Sufism, this intelligent consciousness is known as the consciousness of species. When this consciousness controls the collective values of all species, it is referred as the collective consciousness of the Cosmos. These two consciousnesses are the foundation of the entire Universe and are collectively "Spirits" (*ruh*).

Every person possesses along with an individual consciousness, species and cosmic consciousness. By species, we meant all the individuals from the first day of creation to the current moment. The collection of the feelings of species does not exist in the individual consciousness; instead, it exists in species mind and from there it is transferred to the consciousness.

Example

A person wants to learn to drive. When he pays attention to it and learns the necessary skills and traffic law to operate a vehicle then after a given period he or she is able to operate a vehicle and obtain a license to drive.

This means that that person activated the skill that already existed inside him or her and made it part of his or her consciousness. In the same way that person can learn any skill or trade of his or her own species. This skill is stored in their species-consciousness and from there it transferred into the consciousness and becomes part of it. In the same way when a person wants to awaken the species-mind or cosmic-mind, then he or she can more or less succeed in the effort the way they are successful in activating the species-mind.

When all the feeling of individual consciousness is absorbed into the consciousness of the species then the individual consciousness is dissolved into the consciousness of the species and it makes contact with the collective consciousness of the human species. They can send their thoughts to any person without the help of any outside medium; no matter how far away the other person lives. They can receive thoughts as well. This skill of transfer of thoughts could be used in many aspects of charisma and improvement of the personality. This discipline is commonly referred as telepathy. When the individual consciousness progresses to a point where it is in harmony with the cosmic consciousness, then they are able to become aware of the collective consciousness of all creatures. Actions and attributes of animals, plants, and angels can be accessed. Planets and star systems can be observed as well.

When the individual consciousness of any person enters the species-consciousness and after that, the cosmic consciousness, then they can study the entire Universe. Since the Universe is dominated by a single consciousness, every wave is aware of the other though they may be at the opposite ends of the Universe. Therefore, if we, through our focus, let the consciousness be immersed into these two consciousnesses then we can understand them just as we are aware of our own conscious feelings and states.

Through higher mental concentration, we can observe the planets and stars of our Universe. Humans, animals, jinns, angels, actions, lifestyles, and the inner realm of plants can be studied and observed as well. The continuing practice of Muraqaba improves the concentration and the individual consciousness, and after being dissolved into the cosmic consciousness sees and hears everything and records it in the memory.

11
Concept of Unity

Consciousness is the inner light (*nur batin*). In order to access this inner light God has sent prophets with Divine Laws (*shariah*). When we contemplate the Divine Laws and the teachings of Prophet Muhammad and try to draw any meaning out of it, then only one truth comes to light and it is that the reason for the creation of human race was to recognize God as a single being. This oneness of God is labeled as *tawheed* (Unity). *Tawheed* or the concept of believing in one God and to declare God as the sole Creator was revealed to prophets and apostles through Divine Revelation (*vahii*). Since prophets receive this revelation through *vahii,* hence whatever statement they make is free of assumptions. On the other hand, religious groups that do not recognize prophets attempt to find and define this Divine Unity through assumptions. Ever since humans appeared on this earth, they have been trying to recognize a single source of authority by seeking directions through assumptions. Religious groups that do not recognize prophets and apostles always tried to seek Unity through conjecture.

Their misguided assumption always presented the concept of Divine Unity through pagan beliefs and these ideologies sometimes clashed with others concepts and religions as well. Any ideology borne out of assumption or fiction can only stand and support other ideologies for a short while, but eventually it fails because it is an ideology based on supposition. On the other hand, the concept of Divine Unity presented by the prophets is not based on postulation.

When we discuss humanity and wish for its welfare then we have to come to the conclusion that the human race is a family. The head of this family is the One, who is beyond any doubts and suspicions.

To unite the human race to this ideology we have to assemble into one idea or a thought. That point of thought is that God is such a Being, Who is the guardian of human race. All the prophets from Adam to Moses to Jesus to Muhammad have preached this Unity of God. The teachings of these prophets do not clash with each other. If the human race wishes to achieve its salvation by unifying into one concept, it has to apply the concept of Unity of God put forth by the prophets.

40

History informs us that the ideologies other then Unity of God put forth by His prophets either have gone with their followers into oblivion or are going through that process.

Today's generations are gloomier then the previous ones and the future generations will be subject to more hopelessness unless the human race eventually goes back to the point of Divine Unity, as introduced by the prophets.

In today's world, we see that different countries and nations have different ways of life, different cultures, dress, and cuisine. It is almost impossible that the physical appearance and activities of the entire human race could become one. However, when we see beyond the physical appearance, into the inner Self then we see that beneath the physical differences, members of human race do have a common spiritual denominator. It is the belief that all creatures are one and the Being that meets the need of creatures is also One. All the advancement, development of the human race, and branches of knowledge are linked to that single Source. No branch of knowledge could become knowledge unless a Being inspired that knowledge in the human mind.

No advancement on any subject is possible without deep thinking. We have to have something to develop otherwise development could not be achieved. Similarly, advancement is only possible when the human race exists. Without it, no advancement could be achieved. Unless an idea to invent something enters the mind, nothing could be invented. This is that link, which is spiritually active in all the species and in every individual of these species. Its source is nothing but the Divine Unity.

What today's scholars need to do is to correct all the wrong interpretations and ideologies. This is the only way to bring nations of the world into one spiritual circle. This spiritual circle is the concept of Divine Unity presented by the Scriptures including the *Qur'an (Koran)*. In order to access the Divine Unity (*tawheed*) of the *Qur'an (Koran)* and to implement it, all prejudices have to be put aside. We have to free ourselves from hatred. The time is not far when the human race after going through the dreadful conflicts of the future whether they are ideological or economic, will be forced to look for survival. Salvation could not be achieved from anywhere except from Divine Unity.

12

Muraqaba and Religion

Members of the religious establishment often declare Muraqaba (meditation) to be something outside of religion. They also claim that it could not be found in Scriptures. This whole argument may impress some one with marginal a mind but when we look at this matter with wisdom and depth, the earlier notion simply melts away. When we look into the teachings of Scriptures including the *Qur'an* (Koran), we find that their main message is for us to contemplate.

Contemplation means to explore with all the mental capabilities the numerous signs scattered all over the Universe. The second main institution of religion is prayer (*salat*). *Salat* is a very broad term which literally means to form a connection. Here it means that through contemplation a person is able to form a connection with the Divine. Contemplation is Muraqaba.

Muraqaba could not be limited to a specific pose because Muraqaba in essence is a mental activity or state. The system of rules and regulation put forth by religion has room for both outward and inward inspirations. Every pillar and activity has its outward (*zahir*) form as well as an inward (*batin*) or meaningful state. Both sides are equally important.

Through obligatory religious acts the most desired inward state is the station of *ihsaan* (higher awareness). The prophet Muhammad has defined *ihsaan* in these words:

> "When you perform *salat*, do it in such a way as if you
> were beholding God or that He were watching you."

Through the inward state (contemplation) of religion when someone achieves that higher level of God-awareness (*ihsaan*), he or she is then able to gain gnosis of God.

During the time of the prophet Muhammad, the faithful had his glorious company. The spirits of his companions were enlightened with his love. Most of their time was spent in the contemplation on his personality and essence. They were always busy finding the wisdom through his words and actions. Because of this focused life, they were able to gain the spiritual awareness. Moreover because of his company they had involuntarily gained the cognitive and intuitive angle of perception without much effort.

After his physical demise, the source of guidance was removed from the outward sight. Gradually the inward (*batin*) side of religion lost the prominence it had once enjoyed. Islam then turned into a collection of outward rituals and traditions. *Ahlul Bayt* and later Sufi saints then tried to popularize the *inner* mode of religion and created a system (*silsila*; Sufi orders) through which gaining that awareness was made possible. Its purpose was to combine *dhikr* (remembrance) with *fikr* (contemplation). The practical form of *fikr* was then labeled as Muraqaba, which means to think or to focus on a given object.

Contemplation:

Generally in all religious scriptures and especially in the *Qur'an (Koran)*, noesis or contemplation is greatly emphasized. In various verses cognition is even ordered, for examples there are verses that dictate to contemplate on skies, on the land, or on rain and the growth of plants, and in some on the birth of animals as well as humans is stressed. Through various styles of suggestions, it is stressed to make deep thinking part of regular life. According to the *Qur'an* (Koran), those who possess knowledge and those who are nearer to God are immersed in deep thinking.

God has stated in the *Qur'an (*Koran*)*:

> "In the creation of earth and skies and in the daily routine of day and night, there are signs for those wise people who remember God, standing, sitting and resting and those who contemplate on the creation of skies and earth and as a result come to conclusion that O' Our Lord, Thou has not created these with no purpose." [*aal-imran*}

Besides the universe, the *Qur'an* (Koran) has also disclosed the Divine Essence and Attributes, as in these verses:

> "Wherever you turn, you see the Face of God."
> "Be aware, be certain that God is seeing you."
> "God engulfs everything."

It is stated in the *Qur'an* (Koran):

> "Did you not see that person (Ezra) who was walking by a city (Jerusalem) the roofs of which had collapsed. Said he, How would God revive that city after it has been completely destroyed? So God kept him dead for a hundred years and then gave him back life. God said, since how long have you stayed here. He replied, maybe a day or two. God said nay. You were dead for a hundred years. Look at your food and drink, has it not been decayed? Look at your mule. We did that to show you Our sign for the people. And watch these bones how We are going to connect them. Then We will dress them with flesh. Then when the Reality was revealed to him he said, 'now I know that God is omnipotent.'"
>
> [*al-Baqara*]

In Sura aal-Imran it stated:

> "And no man is entitled to converse with Him unless through *vahii* or behind a Veil or through a messenger, who communicates with whatever He wishes. Verily, He is all-glory and all-Wise. And in the same way We sent you Our Word through *vahii*. You were not aware of what Book is and what faith is. But We made that Book a light (*nur*), and We guide whomever We wish."

It is stated in *Sura* Mulk:

> "He, who created seven skies on top of each other, you would not be able to find any error in the creative work of the Merciful. See it again. Have you found any fault? Look at it again and again, your sight would return back to you after having failed, it would be tired as well."
>
> "In fact these are the bright verses(*ayat*) which are saved in their bosoms, those have been given the knowledge. And no one could deny Our verses except the unjust." [*Sura* Ankaboot]

> "We attest on the places where stars fall. If could perceive, it is a great consecration. No doubt, this *Qur'an* (Koran) is glorious, saved in a book which is protected. No one can touch it, except those who are pure. It is revealed from the Lord of the Worlds."

In *Sura* Rahman (Merciful) there is an invitation to think:

> "O' throng of humans and jinns! If you have the power
> to cross the boundaries of the Universe, then do so. You
> could not except through Sultan (spiritual ability)."

In *Sura* Baqarah, it is stated,

> "Let it be followers of Islam, Jews or Christians or Sabi,
> whoever has faith in God and on the Day of Judgement
> and do good deeds, their reward is saved with their
> Lord. They have no fear nor do them grief."

In all of the above verses wherever a hidden realm is mentioned, the purpose is to implant these facts in the person's consciousness, so that not even a trace of doubt stays thereafter. Thereby that person reaches the level of faith (*iman*). This faith takes the person to the level of observation. According to Sufi Saints, this level is the attestation of the heart that comes after the verbal affirmation of faith. The idea is to make them aware of the vision of their heart through which they will be able to witness matters that are the foundation of the faith (*iman*).

In order to achieve this level of faith and to make it part of the consciousness, Sufi Saints have always recommended Muraqaba to their students. Through Muraqaba, reality is imposed on the heart in a way that the vision of the soul is activated and the person witnesses the reality in its form before them.

By analyzing cognition, we come to a realization that cognition is a mental process in which a person is able to concentrate deeply on any given idea, point or observation after surrendering all other unrelated thoughts and whims. When the Sufis and other Masters of Spirituality gave this contemplation a form of exercise and made rules and regulations then it was termed as Muraqaba, Meditation or *Ga'yan* (as in Buddhist or Hindu mysticism).

In human cognition there exists a light that can observe the inner dimension (*batin*) of any outward object (*zahir*) or the hidden state (*ghayb*) of a being. The observation of the hidden realm (*ghayb*) could declassify any being of the outward (*zahir*). In other words when we witness the hidden reality of any being then its outward form could no longer be hidden from us. Through this process the limits of the outward is revealed to the human consciousness and it becomes increasingly possible to learn where the outward had originated.

This is the way of the prophets of God that they locate the outward through the inner. By contemplating into the inner, the mind eventually can be lit by that light which reveals the hidden realities into observation. Prophet Muhammad has called this light the Light of Insight (*nur-firasat*).

There is a saying (*hadith*) of the Prophet:

> "Fear the insight of the faithful (*mo'min*) for he sees through the Light of God."

The concentration of thought is imperative in both the outward (academic) and esoteric studies. Until the desire, enthusiasm, curiosity and depth are created, we are unable to learn any branch of knowledge. In the same way in order to learn the spiritual science it is necessary that a person be able to focus all of his or her mental abilities on one point. When a person contemplates with the help of strong will and purity of actions then the Point of Cognition (*nuqta-e-fikr*) is activated and its meaning and its inner dimensions manifest themselves.

On numerous occasions in the *Qur'an* (Koran), God has shown His signs and has directed to contemplate on those signs. A sign is in fact a name of outward motions or manifestations and the the focus on contemplations shows that there are those hidden factors whose complete understanding would lead humans towards the Truth. Actually, all physical sciences and beings are based on Spiritual Laws. Through contemplation and concentration, the knowledge of those laws can be accessed.

The Prophet Muhammad has said:

> "The one who gains awareness of himself gains awareness of God."

Human Soul, Ego or Spirit is a collection of such attributes that represents the entire cosmos. That is why man is also known as microcosm (*a'lam asghar*). When someone tries to gain awareness of the Self and the attributes of his soul then the Laws of Creativity are revealed to him. Self-awareness eventually creates such energy in the mind that it becomes a basis of the awareness of the Creator.

God says in the *Qur'an* (Koran):

> "We are closer to you than your cardinal vein."
> "He is inside your soul. Why don't you see?"
> "We will soon reveal to them Our signs in the cosmos and in the souls."

The right way towards self-awareness has been transferred from the Prophets and Apostles to the Mankind. Among the different methods applied by those who were blessed with prophethood (*nur-e-nabuwat*), Muraqaba is the most prominent.

Muraqaba is an act of the Heart. The word itself came from the Arabic word *raqeeb*. *Raqeeb* is one of the Divine Names listed in the *Qur'an* (Koran) and its literal meaning is protector or caretaker. This indicates protecting the mind from the negative and worrying thoughts and focusing on God or His attributes or signs.

In Sufi terminology, Muraqaba means to contemplate or to imagine. The eighteenth century Indian Sufi Syed Shah Waliullah Muhadith Dehlevi (1702-1762) wrote:

"The truth about Muraqaba is to let the force of perception concentrate on an object or idea, whether it is Divine Attributes or on the separation of body and soul or any other topic. This attention should be such that all the intelligence, whims, thoughts and all the senses become dormant to this focus. And the thing that does not feel becomes known without ever being felt."

It means that in the human senses, the knowledge that is beyond the scope of intelligence and consciousness and is part of the soul, after having crossed the boundaries of senses and perception enters the field of observation and inspection through Muraqaba.

Another Indian Sufi, Syed Ghauth Ali Shah (1804-1880) wrote in his book *Taleem Ghauthia*, "One of the conditions of Muraqaba is that the person's attention always remains at his heart. He is always immersed in the state of his heart. The second condition is to keep his focus on the one of the Divine Names or any verse of the *Qur'an* (Koran). The focus should be increased to a point where the person himself becomes the meaning and becomes unaware of self. Keep in mind that Muraqaba is based on the state of the heart. When the heart is attentive to God or anything other than God then all internal organs follow its command, because they are all obedient to the heart. The final stage of the Muraqaba is when the person is so immersed in imagining the Beloved that he becomes totally unaware of all else."

Another Sufi Ibn Mubarak once said to someone, "Raqib Al-Lah. When that person asked him what it meant, he replied," Always live as if you are seeing God."

The prophet Muhammad once said, "Pray to God as though you are watching Him. And if you could not do that, imagine that He is watching you." In this saying of the Prophet (*hadith*) the first station is observation while the second is Muraqaba.

Imam Ghazali (d.1150) in his book *chemia sa'adat* wrote:

"O' friend, do not think that the door of the heart toward spiritual realm does not open before death. This idea is wrong. When a person during his wakefulness, prays and abstains from immoral behavior, seeks solitude, closes his eyes and after suspending the outward senses turns his heart towards Gnosis. And then instead of using the tongue, invocate (dhikr) the Divine Name of Al-Lah, with his heart and then loses himself and surrenders from all the physical things of this world. Then after reaching this station, the door of his heart opens even during wakefulness. Moreover, what other people see in their dreams he sees with his open eyes. He sees angels, he meets Prophets of God and receives their blessing (faidh)."

In order to observe the hidden realm, all the saints, prophets and apostles have applied cognition and spent months or years with their abilities practicing Muraqaba. It should not be assumed that prophethood can be achieved merely by trying. This is a special privilege that God bestows on a chosen few. The system of prophethood and apostlehood has ended, however revelation (*il'haam*) and awakening of consciousness (*roshan zameeri*) continues.

Abraham

When the prophet Abraham was growing up there came a moment during the search for the truth when he became deeply contemplative. During this gnostic phase of the search for the Beloved, his mind at first turned to the outward objects and toward the very thought of who his Creator was and where He was. That became a focal point of his quest. The depth of the awareness finally created a way towards gnosis and he directly received the Divine Guidance (*hidaya*). In the *Qur'an* (Koran), the quest of Abraham is related as follows:

> "And We let Abraham observed the creatures of the skies and earth so that he could become the man of absolute faith. And when the darkness of the night prevailed, he saw a star. Said he, this is my Lord. So when it fell said he, I do not love those who go down.
> "Then when he saw the moon, the bright, and glowing, said he, this is my Creator. When that fell too Abraham said, if my God would not guide me then I would be among those who have gone astray. Then when saw the sun, he said, this is my God. This is the biggest one. So when that went down, he said, O' my people, no doubt I

am disgusted with your infidelity. I turn my way
towards the One who created this earth and the skies
and I am not among those who worship idols."

[*Sura* Inaam]

Moses

After freeing the Israelites from the slavery of Pharaoh, Moses on his
way towards the Promised Land spent some time in the Sinai Desert.
There he left his brother Aaron in charge of the community and went
towards what is known today as Mount of Moses (*jabal al musa, koh-e-
toor*) on God's Will. There, he spent forty days and forty nights and
received the Torah.

This event is mentioned in the *Qur'an* (Koran) in these words:

> "And We promised Moses thirty nights and added ten
> more nights, then the period of your Lord was complet-
> ed with forty nights."

Moses spent the entire forty days and nights there but what is interesting is that God only used the term 'night' but the day was not even
mentioned. According to Sufism, 'night' is the name of those senses
(*nocturnal senses*) that are responsible for the hidden revelations.
During Muraqaba, the human senses are influenced by the nocturnal
senses and the person is then able to observe the world after freeing
himself from the clutches of Time and Space. During those forty days
and nights, Moses was dominated by the nocturnal senses and therefore
his mind was able to witness the hidden Reality and Divine Messages.

Mary (The Mother of Jesus)

The Mother of Mary had prayed to God that if she had a child, she
would dedicate him to the Solomon's Temple of Jerusalem. She was
expecting that she would bear a boy; instead, she gave birth to a daughter (Mary). Acting on her promise to God that she would devote Mary to
the Temple, she sent Mary to live in the Temple and her Uncle Prophet
Zachariah (father of John the Baptist) became her custodian. Her reclu-
sive life (*khilwat*) was for achieving mental concentration (Muraqaba).
During her stay she involuntarily began performing miracles and other
supernatural acts. In the *Qur'an* (Koran), it is mentioned that whenever
her Uncle Prophet Zachariah would go to see her in the Temple, he
would be surprised to see fruits of other seasons. Upon inquiring, she
would say that that was the gift from the Lord.

Jesus

Jesus spent forty days in the wilderness praying. During his stay, He was tempted by Satan, who used greed and other tactics to lead him astray. However, Jesus paid no attention to his follies. Eventually Jesus was able to receive the divine favors.

In the Gospels (*injeel*) of Mark, it is stated:

> "And it came to pass in those days that Jesus came from Nazareth of Galilee and was baptized of John in Jordan. And straightway coming up out of the water, saw the heavens opened, and the Spirit like a dove descending upon him. And immediately the Spirit driveth him into the wilderness. And he was there in the wilderness for forty days, tempted of Satan; and was with the wild beasts; and the angels ministered unto him." [1:9-13]

Whether it is a spiritual confinement of Mary or retreat of Moses or Jesus, the main thing is that these noble personalities did spend a part of their life isolated from civilization and worldly affairs and were drawn to the unseen world with their full concentration.

Now we are going to shed some lights on how Muraqaba is related in Islam and its place in the life of the prophet Muhammad.

Cave of Hira

A major turn in the life of prophet Muhammad came when he started to retreat monthly for few days at a cave around three miles away from the city of Mecca. After spending a few days there on his own he would return to his home and family in Mecca. He would take with him food and water as well. Food consisted of dates and crushed beans.

Evidently, he was going there to achieve mental concentration, as this happened before the declaration of prophethood and at that time there existed no system of prayer among the small number of monotheist Arabs for praying to the True God. According to the Sufi point of view, he was using the retreat to practice Muraqaba. During his stay his mind would contemplate the mysteries of the Universe and the Divine Essence. When that concentration reached its zenith, he started witnessing the unseen. First, he saw a group of angels and then he saw Archangel Gabriel. Through Gabriel, his Prophetic training started which culminated in a stage in which he started receiving the command directly from the Divine. This was related in the story of *meraj* in the *Qur'an* (Koran):

"Pure is the Essence which took His servant at night from the Mosque of Mecca (*masjid al-haram*) to the Mosque of Jerusalem (Dome of the Rock), so that he could witness the signs of Our might."

[*Sura* Bani Israel]

"He teaches, He is all-powerful. Appeared in the true face, when at the supreme height. Came closer and further closer. Descended, until the remaining distance was less than two aeches, even less. What the heart saw was not illusion." [*Sura* Najam]

Attention to God

On one occasion when Prophet Muhammad finished his Muraqaba at the cave of Hira, he was given a commandment:

"O' who covers with clothes! Spend thy night in vigil but a small portion, meaning the half night or even smaller portion. Or increased slightly from half and recite the *Qur'an* (Koran) very clearly. We are going to descend a heavy order on thee."

[*Sura* Muzammil]

During the hours of night when the outward senses get groggy and the inner senses are activated, Prophet Muhammad used to keep night vigil. Because of long hours of standing, his feet would get swollen.

With increased mental concentration and physical awakening, this vigil made the strong link even greater, which he had with the unseen world and God. The higher his concentration went, the more he received the observation of the unseen realm and his spiritual growth.

He received another commandment:

"Sever from the rest and focus on Him, the Lord of the East and of the West."

In Sufism, this attempt in which all mental aptitudes are turned toward God is known as Muraqaba of the Divine Essence (*al-dhat*). In the *Qur'an* (Koran) it is stated on several occasions that to create a connection with the Divine. is the sole objective behind all the prayers and exercises, whether it is *salat*, fasting, *zakat* (charity) or *hajj* (pilgrimage), *dhikr* (remembrance of God) or any other form of prayer.

Imam Ali ibn abi Talib has said:

"The foremost in religion is the Gnosis (*ma'arifa*) of Him, the perfection of Gnosis is to testify (*shahada*) of Him, the perfection of testifying of Him is to believe in His Unity (*tawheed*), the perfection of believing in His Unity is to regard Him pure. He is a Being but not through the phenomenon of coming into being. He exists but not from non-existence. He is with everything but not in physical nearness. He is away from everything but not in physical separation. He acts but without connotation of movements and instruments. He sees even when there is none to be looked at from among His creation. He is Single, such that there is none with whom He may keep company or whom He may miss in their absence."

[Nahjul Balagha: Sermon 1]

"These are the people whom the trade and business of worldly life could not distract them in their remembrance (*dhikr*) of God."

[*Sura* Nur]

Religion has established the structure of prayers by keeping in mind the physical and spiritual needs of humans. Connection with the Divine, *dhikr*, imagining His omnipresence, establishing *salat*, imagining God as the sole existence through self-negation, fasting, detachment (*istaghna*), these are all the media through which the mental focus is established on one point and that point is the Essence(*dhat*) of God, who is the Ultimate Reality (*haqiqat kubra*) of this Universe.

In order to have this focus on God and to purify the heart, religion has established the obligatory system of prayers. In addition to that a person may add more non-obligatory (*nafil*) prayers depending on conditions and ability. The night vigils, *dhikr*, recitation of the *Qur'an* (Koran), non-obligatory fastings are used for this purpose. The cognition (*fikr*) is evident in all the prayers and activities. When attempts to achieve cognition are activated, and strengthened then the evil thoughts weaken, and the focus on God deepens. When someone achieves this ecstasy during prayers, the real benefits of prayers are gained.

Prayer and Muraqaba

Just like all other Prophets before him, the prophet Muhammad also devised a system of prayers based on Divine Commandments. This system was devised so that people of all levels of society and ability could perform it and because of that could establish a connection with God. After Unity (*tawheed*), prayer (*salat*) is the most important pillar of Islam. *Salat* reinforces the idea of God's omnipresence and by simply repeating it creates God-awareness. In the *salat* all the movements of daily life are assembled so that a person, no matter what he is doing, remains at the higher level of God's awareness.

Regarding prayer the prophet Muhammad has said,

> "While performing the prayer, feel as if you are witness-ing God or that He is watching you."

This above statement shows that the purpose of the prayer is to have full mental focus on God. Hence the prayer (*salat*) is not just the physi-cal activity and the uttering of certain words. In the prayer, *qayam* (standing), *ruku* and *sajada* (prostration) and recitation are physical aspects while attention directed toward God is the spiritual one. In its essence *salat* (prayer) is a combination of both the physical and spiritu-al activity. Just as physical activity is essential, mental focus is necessary as well. Performing prayer by combining these two factors with full con-centration is what establishing prayers (*qayam us salat*) means. Based on the definition of Muraqaba already given in earlier chapters, we can say that the *salat* (prayer) is that kind of Muraqaba in which along with the physical activity, awareness of God is envisaged. When a person always performs prayer with the above mentioned protocol then the Divine Lights (*anwaar e'lahii*) starts to store in his inner being and this storage of the Lights enables him for his spiritual flight.

Dhikr and Contemplation

According to the teachings of the *Qur'an* (Koran), *dhikr* (remem-brance) of God is highly regarded. In the *Qur'an* (Koran) as well as in *hadith*, *dhikr* is recommended on several occasions. *Salat* is also referred as *dhikr* and its stated purpose is to establish the *dhikr* of God.

The literal meaning of *dhikr* is the act of remembering. It could also mean mentioning because to mention someone is to remember him. When you mention someone and his or her attributes, that act connects you mentally with the person you are mentioning. To remember some-one or mention someone verbally are interrelated. In daily life there are several examples, for instance, when someone is in love with the other person then that love is manifested in way that not only they mention their lover's name but in their heart the thoughts of the beloved prevail as well.

The center of religious teaching is the Essence of God and its purpose is to establish a link between the created and the Creator. In addition, it is to strengthen that relationship to a point where the heart ccan witness the Divine Light (*tadjalli*). Therefore, all functions, whether they are physical or rational are connected with the Divine so that consciously and subconsciously the thought of God encircles the mind.

The first stage of *dhikr* is to repeat continuously (as in mantra) any Divine Name (*ism e'lahi*) or attributes with the tongue. When someone is engaged in this activity, then his or her mind also remains focused on that thought. Even when temporarily the mind disengages in *dhikr* occasionally the mechanical motion never let the will move away from the *dhikr*. This stage in Sufism is referred as *dhikr lisani* (verbal), which means to repeat any Divine Name verbally while maintaining the focus on *dhikr*.

When you say the same name repeatedly then that single thought registers in the mind. Concentration is enhanced and the mind is able to maintain a focus on a single thought. When this occurs then the person feels a burden in repeating the Name with the tongue. He feels pleasure in repeating the Name in the realm of thought (*alam khiyal*). Therefore he switches from *dhikr lisani* to *dhikr khafi* (hidden). This stage in Sufism is known as *dhikr qalbi* (by heart).

Then comes a moment when the person even feels a burden with the *dhikr* by heart as well. At that point the thought of that Name encircles him and he becomes totally immersed in the archetypal world of imagination (*alam al-mithal*). This state is called *dhikr roohi* (spiritual); its other name is Muraqaba. Muraqaba in this case is defined as a thought of God established in such a way that focuses on, and never deviates from Him.

We will explain this entire concept in an analogy. When someone does a *dhikr* of the Divine Name of *al-Qadeer*; at first he would do the *dhikr* by tongue, at the next level he would do the *dhikr* silently by heart, not by his tongue (hence no sound is generated). At the third level he does not have to repeat it by heart, instead the Divine Name *al-Qadeer*, in the form of thought and imagination encircles his mind. This level or style of *dhikr* where a person maintains the imagination of the meaning of the Name is known as Muraqaba. The purpose of all the different styles of *dhikr* is to create a capability in that person so that his entire focus is fully immersed in any one of the Divine Names.

In the beginning the person maintains the thought during the Muraqaba but with continued focus this thought dominates his consciousness along with the entire mental and physical functions. He is able to form a continued relationship with God, and no time is passed where he is not in that state of Muraqaba. When this state of Muraqaba becomes part of the consciousness then his soul ascends towards *alam al-malakut* (world of Platonic intelligence) and he is rewarded with *kashaf* (vision) and *ilhaam* (revelation).

World Religions

There are five major religions in the world today, Hinduism, Buddhism, Judaism, Christianity and Islam. In the teaching of all of these religions or in the life of their founders, Muraqaba plays a major part. In the case of Christianity we have already discussed the Muraqaba of Jesus. Jesus has also said, "Kingdom of God lies inside thee, find it within thyself."

Moses spent forty nights doing Muraqaba at the Mount of Moses (*jabal al-musa*) in Si'nai. In Islam and in the life of the prophet Muhammad we have already mentioned the Muraqaba at the cave of Hira. *Bhagavad Gita* is the holy book of Hinduism. In it a dialogue between Krishna and Arjuna is recorded, which they had before the *Battle of Mahabharata*.

Arjuna asked Krishna,

> "You have talked about having control over one's mind (Muraqaba), you have also talked about self-realization, but I have found my mind to be utterly confused."

Sri Krishna replied,

> "What you are saying is correct. But by using the right resources, and through detachment, and with continued *gayan* (Muraqaba), a confused mind can be focused."

Yoga is derived from Hinduism. Some 2,300 years ago in his book *yoga savitra*, Patanjali Maharishi presented the philosophy of Yoga. In Yoga, various exercises for improving human health and the details about Muraqaba to activate spiritual abilities are collected. Yoga is a word from Sanskrit and its literal meaning is to meet or meeting, whereas *asana* means to sit. Yoga Savitra means exercise. There are a total 84 different *asana* of Yoga. Many of these *asana* were created after observing the postures of different animals. Yoga exercises help improve immunity in the body against diseases and they are a source for purifying the soul.

Muraqaba also played a major part in the life of Siddhartha Guatama Buddha. When Buddha left his kingdom in search of Reality, he spent six years in tough training and eventually did Muraqaba under a tree near Gaya, India. He spent forty days continuously in Muraqaba in search of the Truth. Finally, on the thirty-ninth night he received Enlightenment. There are eight basic points in the teaching of Buddha; the eighth one is the purification of thought and Muraqaba.

13
Benefits of Muraqaba

Just as through physical exercises and other practical ways, like good diet and so on, the physical condition of the body can be improved, in the same way through Muraqaba, mental activities can be improved as well. We are aware of the fact that thoughts and mental conditions have a strong impact on us. When we are scared, we tremble. Our body feels like a weightless mass. On the other hand, vulgar and immoral thoughts leave a person incapable of utilizing his abilities and strength because of a lack of concentration.

Rest is only perceived as lying down, denoting activity in which no energy is used or utilized. However, this description is far from the truth. Many people seem to have peace and tranquility though they may internally be worried and depressed. By having a continuing non-stop flow of thoughts, our energy decreases tremendously. By being overly attached to the web of thoughts, the brain gets tired which results in the waste of stored energy. We all know that mental concentration is a key to good health and that over-worrying weakens the immune system, which results in sickness. This all happens because the waste of energy weakens the immune system and various diseases then attack that person. When a nervous strength gets weaker then the brain becomes slower, memory is affected and weakens.

Due to weak will power, success in life can not be achieved. Life experiences have shown that mental stress eventually leads to diseases and physical ailments. Mental complications directly or indirectly result in heart disease, and gallbladder and kidney stones. Prolonged stress could result in a breakdown of the nervous system. Negative thinking leads to stomach ulcers, hyperacidity (acid reflux) as well as constipation.

To get mental peace most people try those methods that often suspend the consciousness temporarily such as alcohol, drugs, and tranquilizers. These drugs do nothing but create a feeling of self-negation temporarily. These sources not only damage health but also the nervous system and speed up the aging process.

In psychological disorders such as psychosis, life becomes stagnant. Every action has a negative side. The patient feels comfortable in a closed room. He ends all relations and communications with family members. He avoids any contact with other people and becomes insecure. Even in extremely hot weather, the patient tends to sleep with a blanket. Interest in consuming food also declines, and as the consequence the body becomes weak and emaciated.

Schizophrenia

In this state, the influence of the subconscious on the consciousness of the patient increases to such an extent that the patient starts seeing things that are otherwise hidden from the naked eye. Sometimes he sees shadows and other times he sees himself free of physical constraints in the form of a flying shadow. The pressure drawn from this imaginary flying leads some patients to leap from high-rise buildings. They may start hearing voices as well. The patient confines himself to an imaginary world in which he sees beautiful gardens and sees himself as the center of attention of all the residents of the imaginary garden. However, sometimes negative feelings take over and the patient starts crying at some dreadful scene. In other words, his senses fluctuate rapidly. Sometimes he becomes a very intelligent, talented, articulate person while at other times he is senseless and his speech becomes incoherent or gibberish.

Mania

When an attack of mental seizures happens to a mental patient whether it starts slowly or instantly it increases the flow of electrical impulses inside the brain, and since there is no outlet the pressure causes the cell walls to be broken and the outlet somehow opens up. Often when the electrical flow inside the cells decreases to a level of zero (neutral) then the patient suddenly becomes free of any thoughts. Although this is not an ailment, when the space is formed inside the main frame of the brain, the electrical flow concentrates on one side of the cells, to a point when these cells lose all memory. When this happens, the patient no matter how hard he tries to remember an event or thing can not do so. On the one hand, the flow increases to a point where the brain stops functioning. On the other hand, the electrical flow between cells becomes so irregular that the patient becomes irrational. Sometimes he claims prophethood while on other occasions proclaims himself king.

When this condition persists, the patient may become unaware of the need of clothing or food. In some cases, the patient would continue walking endlessly. He even runs but his body never gets tired or fatigued. Sometimes stares endlessly into the space totally engrossed in thoughts. His worldly life becomes inconsistent. The need of rest and luxury goes away as well. His body holds so much energy that he has to be chained for control. The mental patient may keep on talking incoherently. His eyes become shiny and magnetic. Blinking happens very rarely. For psychosis, schizophrenia and mania both major and minor tranquilizers are used which result in the following side effects; dry mouth, weaker eyesight, low blood pressure, weight gain, increase in blood sugar. Some patients also are diagnosed with jaundice. Body temperature rises; Parkinson's disease, paranoia, anxiety, distress, and confusion also are common. With that low appetite sometimes the patient becomes bedridden permanently. Other side effects like these could also happen which may send the patient into a deep coma. Minor tranquilizers are used to keep the mind peaceful and calm.

The other negative effects of these medicines are that the patient becomes dependent on them as well. Prolonged use may also necessitate the increase of dosage since after a while the usual dosage fails to be as effective as the original dose. Tranquilizers should never be stopped instantly as this could lead to other serious ailments such as hysteria, insomnia, nausea, body pain, and loss of concentration, to name a few. On the contrary, if the patient is treated with Muraqaba under medical supervision he gets peaceful and calm. In addition, the negative mentality is also weakened by it and the flow of thoughts becomes uniform. Through Muraqaba, the natural link between mind and spirit is enhanced and the man gets new energy from his own Spirit. The mental state at that time is different from that of wakefulness or sleep. Hence, the deterioration of nervous system stops and the cell division goes back to a normal rate.

Physically there are two systems work in our body; the Sympathetic and Parasympathetic system. The first mentioned system controls the high blood pressure and the dilation of cornea. The latter system handles lowering blood pressure, lowering of heartbeat and contraction of cornea and movement of matter within the body. This system works without our will or discretion. For example we are bound to inhale and exhale. Even if we hold the breath for a few moments eventually we are forced to breathe anyway. Heartbeat is also beyond our control. That is why these days there are some Medical experts and Spiritual scientists working to devise a method or exercise through which we would be able to control the functioning of the Parasympathetic System to defend ourselves against diseases and ailments and some diseases may even be eliminated altogether. On this basis, scientists have created a system called 'Bio Feed Back' on which research is underway.

Through Muraqaba, the parasympathetic system could be controlled at will. Muraqaba brings good changes in the system. The feeling of Muraqaba takes us toward deeper calm and stillness. This state otherwise does not stay with us because the mind never stays on anything for too long. Muraqaba not only increases the will power but physically and psychologically numerous benefits are achieved as well. Experiences and observations have shown that following physical and psychological benefits are achieved by practicing Muraqaba.

_ Control of blood pressure.
_ Increase in life expectancy.
_ Improvement in eyesight (vision).
_ Reduction of fat in blood.
_ Enhanced creativity.
_ Less irritability.
_ Improvement in the performance of heart.
_ Improvement in hearing.
_ Increased immunity.
_ End of depression and anxiety.
_ Reduction of stress.
_ Increase of red blood corpuscles.
_ Improved memory.
_ Better decision making.
_ End of insomnia and deeper sleep.
_ End of fear, increase of levity.
_ End of doubt.
_ End of enmity and jealousy.
_ After the success of Muraqaba a person is set free from the fear of witchcraft, ghosts, and all negative thoughts.

14
Levels

To gain self-awareness and to awaken spiritual abilities, Muraqaba should be practiced consistently. Through Muraqaba, our hidden qualities slowly surface and we eventually gain self-awareness.

It is our daily observation that when we try to learn a new skill or any form of art or to awaken any latent ability we have to practice using a devised method. Continued practice results in gradual improvement in ability and eventually we acquire that skill. For instance when we try to learn painting, at first with the supervision of a teacher we begin with drawing lines on a paper, which ends up in some kind of a sketch. In the beginning the pencil does not draw what we intend to draw. However, with practice we are eventually able to draw what we are supposed to.

Example:

A newborn infant does not understand the environment in which he lives, the way an adult person does. He sees things but is not able to comprehend their meaning or use. Knowledge of the environment comes slowly in a systematic fashion and intellectual maturity takes years. In the beginning, the child has difficulty in utilizing his abilities. When he starts to walk, he first crawls. Moreover, when he can stand on his feet then for number of months he is unable to balance. It takes the effort of many months before he is able to walk on his own.

Speaking starts with broken words then progresses to incomplete sentences. Often the meanings of words gets mixed up. However, with passing of time a child is able to converse using complete sentences. Together with individual efforts and the help of teachers and parents, the child is eventually able to read and write after spending years learning.

The point we are trying to make is that when any new ability grows, the consciousness absorbs it gradually. Just as a child goes through different stages of learning to acquire full knowledge about any subject, in the same manner, an adult also has to go through various learning levels in order to acquire any new skill. More or less the same condition prevails when someone tries to activate (awaken) esoteric or hidden senses. Since learning hidden senses is a relatively new process for the consciousness, in the beginning it faces some difficulties and challenges in understanding and using them.

It would be premature to assume that as we close our eyes for Muraqaba within a day or two all those observations and experiences would become known that are the essence of Muraqaba. With continued practice and enthusiastic interest, a person gradually journeys through the realm of Muraqaba.

In the beginning, mental focus is hard to achieve. However, with practice it is eventually achieved. The more focus or concentration is enhanced the more hidden senses are activated. Based on the consciousness strength the person goes through the spiritual experiences and esoteric observations. Spiritual state and observation increase with time. Once fully achieved the spiritual abilities can be used at will just as other physical abilities.

During these stages, spiritual students need a spiritual tutor who can teach them almost as if they were kindergarten students, until the student eventually masters his or her own spiritual skills.

The spiritual state and observation varies in every individual and it depends on the spiritual and conscious level of that person. That is why only an experienced Spiritual Master or (murshid) can analyze an individual's spiritual strength. However, depending upon the conscious strength, the different levels or stages that any student goes through are more or less the same. Based on strength and ability the different stages or levels are the following.

Drowsiness

Drowsiness is the earliest stage of Muraqaba. When someone begins the practice of Muraqaba for the first time, often he or she becomes drowsy and goes to sleep. After few days the condition that prevails in the mind can neither be called asleep or awake. This is an interim stage between waking and sleeping. However, the consciousness is not yet aware of that. That is why after the Muraqaba, one feels like he or she saw something but are unable to remember it.

> 1. *I did the Muraqaba at 10:17 pm. I was focused right away. Often I would go into sleep. I felt like I was washing someone's feet. Then during the drowsy state, I saw a black shadow (which was not solid) came out of my body, and was absorbed into the front wall.*
>
> (Akmal, Lahore)

2. During Muraqaba, I visualize Qalandar Baba (founder of Sufi order of Azeemia). During Muraqaba my mind remains focused. However while doing it I sometimes fall asleep. Then a very light image of Qalandar Baba appears and when I try to focus on it, I fall asleep. On average I do Muraqaba for 30 minutes daily. However, except for the initial visualization nothing else registers in my mind. By the grace of God, my mind is much purified now.

(Tahir Jalil)

Under the influence of sleep, I saw that repentance was being taught. On one occasion during Muraqaba, while I was groggy I saw I was meeting with jinns. I felt a little fear. I could not remember the details of the encounter. All day I do the invocation (dhikr) of Ya-Hayi Ya- Qayumu which makes me feel that God is always facing me. During prayers as well, the feeling that God is seeing remains prevalent. Sometimes it leads to ecstasy during which all I want to do is to cry. Once the drowsiness was so strong that I felt that God is omnipresent in every piece of sand of this Universe and then I felt like I no longer exist.

(Nasreen)

Colorful Dreams

After a given period of starting Muraqaba the student usually sees clearer dreams. Sometimes this starts right after going to sleep and continues the entire night. Different scenes come and go in which he sees trees, flowers, greenery, mountains, lush green valleys, lakes, rivers, buildings, birds and so on. These dreams usually have more depth and detail. Even after waking up their effect lasts for a while.

The student sees colorful dreams as well. In these dreams, the vision is more colorful compared to other dreams. After seeing colored dreams, the viewer feels joy, delight and serenity. The reason behind seeing more and clearer dreams is that by practicing Muraqaba, a person's link with his subconscious increases and he is able to receive more and more of the flow of subconscious information. When dreams become deeper, then the person starts seeing more and more 'true dreams' in which future outcome is displayed in actuality rather then symbolically. Whatever that person sees in his dream usually manifests itself after awakening or whatever he sees is proven after he wakes up. Dreams become so clear that interpreting is no longer needed. The person can draw conclusions on his or her own.

Whatever a student sees in his or her dreams, the spiritual master *(murshid)* gives his student lessons based on that. Much spiritual based knowledge is transferred from the Sufi master to that student through dreams.

Using his spiritual power the master cleans the mind of his student. Impurity is washed and converted into subtlety.

This subtlety is gradually transferred from dream stage to awakened stage. Through dreams the spiritual master has his student journey into the spiritual world. In the spiritual world, the students glimpse and have audience with prophets, saints, and other spiritual personalities. Such matters come before observation so that the student has no choice but to remember them. The images of *roya sadiqa* (true dream) are so deep that mind is forced to repeat them.

That is how consciousness achieves strength in keeping the esoteric flow and the *fikr lateef* (subtle cognition) flows in the student for a longer period. By seeing more and more dreams, the interest of the student in learning paranormal studies is also enhanced. He or she starts seeing the kind of dreams that enabled them to avoid future mishaps or ailments (sickness)

The following is a list of dreams sent by students and their interpretations given by the author of this book.

A female student reports:

I am very much interested in learning spiritual studies. Whenever I get a chance, I do Muraqaba. The following is a dream that I saw a couple of days ago.

Dream:
I saw a huge field. In the middle of that field there is a hole similar to a grave. The field is lush green. However, in that grave a red liquid seemed to be present. Within moments, that liquid turned into a huge flame of fire.

Interpretation
The dream is reflecting high blood pressure. You need to check with a gynecologist in order to treat hypertension because it may endanger the life of your unborn baby.

Dream 2:
In our busy life, I try to find time to do Muraqaba for 10-15 minutes. Following is a dream that I see very often.

A goat is being slaughtered and skinned. However, it is still alive but shows no sign of pain or discomfort, though the eyes show sadness. In the same manner, I sometimes see a cow and that cow as well shows no sign of pain but its face reflects injustice. During the dream, I feel their pain and try to run away from it. In real life as well I could not see any animal being slaughtered (like during Eid-ul-Adha)

Interpretation

When there is no hope in life and depression kicks in, it seems like there is no light of hope at all. The subconscious then shows those images during deep sleep.

Hopelessness and disappointment present these symbols in the form of gloomy and sad pictures. These are all the wishes that were not met and the heart does not have enough strength to replace them with new hopes and wishes. Your dream also points to a weaker mind.

Advice

During the pre-dawn hours of the morning for at least half an hour do brisk walking. It helps overcome the weakness of the mind.

Dream 3

I went to sleep right after doing Muraqaba. I saw in the dream that a ball of spaghetti came out of my mouth and my mouth was full of them. Some of them were cooked. I shredded some sugar on them and took them back into my mouth. With the help of my fingers, I forced them inside my throat. Right then I saw myself at a mountain and the rain started right after that. I have seen this dream twice. After getting up early in the morning, I usually get feverish. I have lost my appetite. All day I obsess about that dream.

Interpretation

The dream is pointing towards an ailment that has to do with the digestive system. The last part of your dream suggests that due to unbalanced diet your intestine has become over-sensitive. To see this dream twice suggests that this disorder has not gone away and hence it could not simply be ignored. Needless to say a consultation with your physician and a balanced diet are in order. Otherwise, this could lead to other complications.

Dream 4

After doing the Muraqaba, I lay down and went to sleep right away. I saw that I was told by my parents to polish the cooking pot from the polish shop. I told the person doing the polish that I would be back with my cousin. When I got to home, my mom gave me mango and instructed me to take them to my sister in law. Upon reaching my sister-in-law's home, I was saddened to see her weak and sick. I gave her the mangoes and asked if she could go with me back home. She agreed and we went back home. Then I saw myself strolling somewhere and I have a cooking pot with me. I also saw black stains in my clothes.

Interpretation

Overindulgence of sugar is causing trouble. Proper treatment has not been done yet which led to the outbreak of the disease which sometimes remains dormant. When the next outbreak occurs please see your physician and follow his advice.

Dream 5

I am a retired government officer. I am 65 years old. I do Muraqaba every night for 15 minutes before going to bed. I saw in my dream that my son is getting married even though he is married and saw that his wife is actively involved in his second wedding.

Interpretation

You made a promise to someone but have not fulfilled it. Your conscience is reminding you of your obligation. Listen to your conscience or else you may have a nervous breakdown eventually.

Dream 6

Last night after doing the Muraqaba I went to sleep right away. I saw that my neighbor's house was on fire and the fire eventually reaching our home and part of it was being burnt. I, instead of extinguishing the fire, was wishing that it would grow. My dad warned me not to inflame the fire otherwise the roof would fall and the entire house would be destroyed and that would be a huge loss to us.

Interpretation

This dream is a warning. The person who saw that dream should avoid a behavior that led to a situation in his business and on which he is wrongly insisting. He should rethink and change his behavior.

Dream 7

I often go to sleep after doing Muraqaba. One night I saw in a dream that I have a 4-year-old daughter. My sister-in-law is insisting that I should beat my daughter because she is not pretty. I then grab her hand and my sister-in-law cuts her hand. After that, I sever my daughter's hand. Then after few moments when I see her, I saw that her hands are okay and are attached to her body. Then I saw one of her hands was cut and the other had only one finger and a thumb. I got frightened and start crying and I said to myself how bad I am that I cut the limb of my own daughter.

Interpretation

Symbolic images of backbiting and uncontrolled anger were displayed in the dream. The subconscious is strongly protesting this behavioral pattern. If the guidance of the subconscious is not followed, the consequences will not be pleasant.

Dream 8

Since last Saturday, I have started practicing Muraqaba after the pre-drawn prayers. The other night I saw in my dream that I am going to Karachi. On my way to Karachi, I met several people who stabbed me. My whole body was blooded. Then I saw that they locked me in a room. When I was stabbed, I shouted and cried, however during crying no tears were coming out of my eyes. The place where I was locked there was another man who slaughtered a pony and gave me the flesh. Then I saw that there was a huge jungle in which bears and lions, cheetahs and dogs were roaming freely. They started following me but I was able to ran faster and started flying in the air. When I landed, I was surprised to see that there were no animals around. Then I started to climb a thorny tree and then all of a sudden a bear starts chasing me. Then I climbed a mountain and saw an elephant. The elephant ran away after seeing another man; however, the bear stood there. Then after coming down from the mountain I started attacking the bear with a knife. The bear ran away after that and returned to my city (Multan).

Interpretation

All the different sketches of the dream point to anxiety, insecurity, worries, and ailing health. All these conditions came into being because the person who saw the dream is overly emotional. There is no balance in life. Consumption of food is improper as well.

Dream 9

I usually do Muraqaba daily and try not to miss it. I saw a dream, which I would like you to interpret for me. I saw that it was nighttime. The sky was of light blue color. When I looked up to see the sky I saw bright stars. In the middle of stars was a big moon. Near the moon, there is a fairy standing, wearing a glittery dress. She is wearing a shiny crown and has a white stick in her hand. There are stars in that stick as well and she is smiling at me.

Interpretation

Even since early childhood, you have a habit of thinking and day-dreaming. Due to the overindulgence of that behavior you have become ultra-sensitive. Because of which you have become unhappy and depressed, life seems like a collection of unhappy events. When that condition became serious and the nervous system itself was being a effected then it showed you this pleasant dream so that you may feel lighthearted. The dream you saw must have been quite a while ago because it does not reflect any thing about the practice of Muraqaba that you have been doing.

Dream 10

Even since I started Muraqaba, I have been seeing geometrical figures in my dreams often. Whenever I see them, I get scared. These figures sometimes evolve into a tree.

Interpretation

These figures represent the close friends who spend most of their time in the company of each other. Either they spend time together every day or at least several times in a week. There are a total of six or seven friends. Three of them are naïve and down to earth and nice, however the others are the bad seed. They are the kind of friends who give you wrong advice and are bad influence.

Advice

You have to be very cautions of these friends who give you intentionally wrong advice. Otherwise, you could end up in big trouble. (God forbid)

Dream 11

I have always been interested in learning paranormal sciences. I have seen some dreams in the past few days whose interpretation I am seeking.

1. I was standing at the window of my room and heard Prophet Muhammad reciting the Qur'an (Koran)) in the basement. I said to myself the how beautiful the voice of Prophet Muhammad really is.
2. I saw myself donning white clothes and standing at my school. Standing beside me is the prophet Muhammad who is wearing white clothes as well. There are some people around too. Nearly a big candle is glowing. The prophet Muhammad then said that the time of his death is approaching and angels are descending from heaven. I then started sobbing and said to him not to talk like that and I hold his forearms and

*took him to another room. The other two men also accompanied us.
They were standing right and left of him.*

*3. During the month of Shaban (the 8th Islamic month) I saw myself
strolling in the terrace of my home after bathing. All of a sudden, a
white cloud starts emitting light and falls on the front wall. The light
starts writing the Kalama on the wall. I then started reciting the
Kalama myself. I then called to my mom and sister to come but when
they arrive the light goes off.*

*4. A few days ago, I saw in a dream that it was a nighttime and a full
moon was on the horizon. All of my family was on the roof of my house.
Every one said how lovely the moonlight was. I too liked the moon and
the moment I raised my hand towards it, it came into my hand.*

Interpretation

From early childhood, your ability to learn spiritual sciences was
activated. Nature wants to use your spiritual abilities to assist the mission of Prophet Muhammad and, God willing, you will be able to help
spread his mission. The best thing would be for you to select a spiritual
master who has gone through the ups and down of the spiritual path to
assist you in your spiritual endeavors.

I pray for you that God may make you the source of peace and serenity for His creatures and the medium through which the spiritual mission of Prophet Muhammad is spread across the globe (Amen).

The interpretation of all the dreams that you have seen is what I just
stated above.

Dream 12

*I went to sleep after performing Muraqaba. I saw in my dream
that my husband and I, along with another man and woman were
going somewhere. This woman took us to a desert, took my hand, and
started running. We were running in a circular formation and I felt like
we were sinking in the sands while running. Then I felt as if we were
not the only ones instead there were thousands of men and women.
Every one was holding each other's hand and though sand was up to
their neck, they kept running. I could not tell how exciting it was.
Suddenly I felt like we were circling the Holy Kaaba. It was very dark
but I knew that my family was there too. Though I could not tell which
members of my family were there, I did know that my aunt was there.
Then a white pigeon came and the entire place was lit. In the dark I
could only see that pigeon; then I heard that voice of my aunt asking,
"did (page 29) you know who that pigeon was?" I then asked her who
it was and she said it was Sufi Master Muhammad Zachariah. I woke
up right then. This is the second time in the six months that I have seen
him. In the first dream, I saw his tomb.*

Interpretation

Sufi Master Zachariah was a *Qutb* (see glossary). Since you have seen him in your dream, you are definitely going to get the spiritual blessing (*faidh*) from him. Please arrange for his soul, *Qur'an khuwani* and *lungar* (see glossary).

Dream 13

I have been doing Muraqaba twice: first before going to bed and second, at the predawn hour. I saw in my dream that I am running up the stairs, which are going all the way up the hill. At the hill top there is a tomb of some Sufi master. A few days later, I saw a similar dream of running up the stairs. When I reached the top, there was a shrine of some Sufi master. I was spiritually overwhelmed at the scene. I wanted to enter the shrine but then I woke up.

Before seeing these dreams I saw a long time ago that some Sufi saints were descending from the sky in a jeep, their faces were glowing. They saw me and then went away. Then came back and returned towards the sky in the same jeep.

A couple of years ago when I was in Karachi I saw a dream when after performing the pre-dawn prayers I took a nap. I saw a huge serpent coming towards me. I quickly put a basket made of wood on top of it. Right away, a bright light started coming of that basket.

Interpretation

You have genuine interests in learning spiritual sciences and your Soul is telling you that if you practice with persistence you will eventually succeed. During the period when you saw the dream about the snake and the basket, you had tonsillitis. If you get that again make sure you complete the treatment and the entire course of medicine. A chronic tonsillitis could result in other complications. My experience shows that a chronic tonsillitis could cause polio as well. Using color therapy oil made of yellow lights is the best cure for tonsillitis.

Dream 14

Every night before going to bed, I do Muraqaba of "visualization of Sufi master." One night I saw that a Sufi master (author) called on us at our home. I was so happy that I wished I could tell the whole city. On our roof, there is a pot of roses whose branches extend to our terrace. We all are chatting. Then I informed all my friends that our Sufi shaykh is visiting and they all came to see him. My mom expressed the desire to visit Karachi and the Sufi shaykh invited us as well and said he would send his men to pick us up from the station. Their sign would be that they would be carrying olive oil. Then my younger sister, and I,

Sufi Shaykh went to see our relative and then I shouted, "Look who is here" after seeing the dream my mom woke me up. It was the time of pre-dawn prayers.

Interpretation

The dream will manifest in reality exactly the way you have seen it. In fact, your devotion has activated your inner eye in your dream. May God give you spiritual improvement immensely (Amen)

Dream 15

I went to sleep right after doing Muraqaba and saw in my dream that two lions are sitting in a tall tree. I asked my uncle to bring a gun. While he was searching for the gun, the lions came out of the tree and went into the woods. My two cousins were going towards the woods and I warned them about the lions but they ignored my advice and went anyway. One of them was attacked by the lion and took her feet into its mouth. People were gathered at the scene however no one had the courage to intervene. I went ahead and saved her from the clutches of the lion. She looked at me thankfully. I took her into my arm, and sent her home.

Interpretation

Man is composed of the elements. These elements are in order. God makes the decision of their quantity. Balance is kept in the creation and there is a system of values. In this sense, sexual thoughts are also a gift of nature. There are ways to accommodate it. However to indulge in erotic thoughts way ahead of time and to focus on it constantly is a waste of time and injurious to health as well. Things that come with time and appropriate condition should be acceptable. Man is entitled to desire but is not authorized to impose his will on others. This is what the *Qur'an* (Koran) teaches. Values are based on that we nevertheless surrender to this Divine Rule. All aspects of the dream are pointing towards this.

Dream 16

After doing Muraqaba, I went to bed immediately. I saw in my dream that in the sky words of Al-Lah and Muhammad were written. Surrounding these are flowers in a cloudy way. On my right hand there is a guy and I said to him that if the people or the government asked me to testify about this then I will testify about this. I have seen these two names with my own eyes. I often see myself praying or performing wudu in my dreams.

Interpretation

Beholding the glorious written names of God and the prophet Muhammad in the sky points to the pure and honest beliefs of the beholder. On the other hand, it also refers to success in life and a better future.

Dream 17

I am a student in eleventh grade; it has been three months since I started doing Muraqaba. One night I saw a strange dream whose interpretation I am seeking from you. The dream is as follows:

I am returning home from the house of my tutor. On my way back I looked towards the northeast side of the sky and I saw many moons in the sky and each of them had verses written on them.

I became ecstatic by looking at it. That moment as I turned back to return to my tutor, I saw on the southeast side of the sky the verse of Surah al-rahman of the Qur'an (Koran).

I went straight to my tutor's home. I informed him about it and he came along with me to see it. However, he could not see it. Right then I woke up. I tried to go back to sleep to see that writing one more time but could not.

I related this dream to my tutor the other day and he said it shows that my future is bright. Please interpret the dream for me.

Interpretation

The rule of giving dream interpretation is that once an interpretation is given, any other interpretation of the same dream should not be given. Because after listening to the interpretation the subconscious registers that interpretation. The prophet Muhammad has instructed that dreams can only be related to a person who has some knowledge of the technicalities of giving interpretation. Dreaming is one of the branches of Divine Knowledge (*ilm ladani*). This Divine Knowledge is not one that can be learned in academies. This branch of knowledge is a gift from the prophet Muhammad and is received only through his blessings.

Dreams about the future

Dream 18

I went to sleep right after Muraqaba. In the dream saw that I am in the residence of my maternal grandmother and watching the sky glittering. One of the stars which is red suddenly falls under my feet. Everyone was surprised. Then that star became a grey color bowl. It seemed like that bowl was ancient and sacred.

Interpretation:

The dream is about your future. Your married life will be happy and good. In addition, from your maternal side a spirit will take a physical form and will be a source of pride for the whole family. I pray to God that what this dream is informing us, is fulfilled and no family dispute will ruin it.

Dream 19

For the last month, I have been doing Muraqaba before going to bed. I have seen many dreams so far. Someone donning a white dress came to see my father and silently fetched some documents from the drawer and put them in his pocket and left. My father did not ask him any questions either; then I woke up.

I saw in my dream that in my city a huge market near the main road has been constructed and is now ready for business. I am taken aback by this market. I was wishing that I could climb to the top of the building when I woke up. The next morning I went to see if there was anything out there but there was nothing.

Interpretation

In the first dream those papers symbolize money which you are about to get, out of nowhere. It is going to be a huge amount. Second dream is also similar to the first, which suggests how the money will bring more prosperity.

Dream 20

I perform Muraqaba nightly. The other night I saw in a dream that my four friends and I were sailing. I was the captain of the ship. Suddenly the ocean dried up and the ship came to rest on a mountain on an island. We were all perplexed about how to continue our journey. One of them suggested that after rainfall there would be enough water for the ship to sail away. Shortly afterwards the rain clouds came and with thunder and wind, heavy rain started to fall. There was enough water afterwards that I took the ship out of there and started sailing again.

Interpretation

Four friends are the symbols of many plans and ideas that are stuck in the mind. These plans are for one thing only because all friends are in the same ship. In order to fulfill the plans there were some obstacles, which had caused hopelessness. Then the help came from a hidden source and things were getting better. This is going on for a while. Raining is the symbol of Divine Help. In the end the sailing of ship symbolizes eventual triumph.

15
Subtle Sensations

By doing Muraqaba regularly, certain types of light and waves start gathering inside that person which negate gravity. Because of these lights, the student goes through different states in which gravitational pull does not apply. For example while doing Muraqaba, during walking, sitting or even laying the feeling of weight disappears (weightlessness). Sometimes the person sees self made of light. During Muraqaba, this weightlessness could make the body suspended as well. Person sees self as flying in space. With closed eyes and open eyes as well, lights of various colors are seen. Flashes of light, similar to a camera flash is felt inside the brain. Body sometimes become oversensitive and the electrical flow inside ones body is felt as well. Because of this concentration of lights, sometimes the body gets a shock too. Feelings of peace and serenity get stronger and deeper. Cognitive and problem solving abilities are enhanced. This and other similar conditions and sensations show the colorfulness of the luminous system and the enhancement of spiritual energy.

The following are Muraqaba reports sent to the author by various students:

Report I

When I close my eyes for Muraqaba, milky white light appears around my eyes. During the Muraqaba, thoughts come and go. Sometimes I get groggy and while others only 'Al-Lah' is the focus of attention. Lights of other colors also appear during Muraqaba for example blue, red and so on. When the influx of thoughts increases then I start the *dhikr* of Ya' Haiyu Ya' Qayyumu. After Muraqaba, different things happen. Sometimes my body feels very light, other times a lot heavier. Sometimes I do not feel like I have a body. Sometimes I feel like my body has moved upward. I also feel a sensation in my brain. Those sensations are pleasant in nature. During Muraqaba, these pleasant sensory waves engulf the brain. My brain gets intoxicated and I usually get to deep sleep afterwards. Occasionally it feels like a dreamy stage. On one occasion, my whole body defying gravity moved upward. I lost awareness of the surrounding. Often during Muraqaba, even the process of inhaling and exhaling felt like interference. Occasionally I see images of my *murshid* (author), also during Muraqaba, I visit various places, and those scenes are so beautiful that writing about them is virtually impossible

(Haroon Ahmed, Lahore)

Report II

At the start of Muraqaba, I saw a *circle (chakra)* of greenish-yellow light then I felt like my bed and I were shaking. For a short while an eye made of light appeared near my right eye. My head and shoulder felt heavier and body was pulled upward. Dark shadows appeared before my eyes. Once a very red light appeared. I felt something in my back, which went all the way to the back of my head. I felt great as if under the magnetic influence of something.

I Did Muraqaba for fifteen minutes. I was able to focus on the image. Throughout it felt like falling drops of rain, especially in my head. The sensation was so strong that I felt like these drops were making holes in my head. I was so focused on that thought that I became unaware of my body. I saw a big door had opened up towards the north, white light was coming out of it, and that light was falling on my body. Then a rain of light started to fall from the sky. I could feel the rain in the right side of any body suddenly the rain increased and the light fell on my body so intensely that I felt a shock in my body.

(Misbahuddin, Karachi)

Report III

I did Muraqaba after pre-dawn prayers and saw myself as a statue of pure light and rings of pure light were encircling me. I felt as I had two bodies, one, which was myself, and the other of pure light.

In addition to these, I am also experiencing certain changes in me. For instance, when someone is about to address me I somehow become aware of it ahead of time and whatever he or she is about to say, also comes to my mind. Secondly if wish to meet someone, that person somehow is able to contact me on his or her own. Thirdly if a big event or incident is about to happen, I get somewhat uneasy prior to that.

(Aslam, Mangla Dam)

Idraak (awareness)

I continued the practice of Muraqaba, eventually overcoming drowsiness. The reason behind getting drowsy is that in the beginning, the consciousness is simply overwhelmed by the influx of inner lights.

When consciousness is no longer influenced by the drowsiness and the mind remains active then the flow of inner or esoteric information gets underway. The student is able to comprehend these spiritual phenomena through cognition. Awareness is a thought that even though is delicate has a form.

Speed of mind meets its form. For example, when someone say "apple", the picture of apple does appear in the mind. These pictorials are so light, the sight could not see it; however, senses do encompass it. Sometimes hidden information comes in the form of a voice. The voice is usually of low decibels but it manages to explain the incoming news or the vision.

Report IV

I gained focus right after starting Muraqaba. I felt as if the waves of thoughts were entering through my ears. Whenever an image appears it's sounds are heard as well.

(M. Salam)

Report V

During Muraqaba, I hear noises as if tidal waves are colliding with the coastline. After few days, I heard the sound as if someone were talking. It was not the sound that we normally hear, the one that comes through our ears; instead, this sound came from within. One day during Muraqaba, someone called my name, when I opened my eyes, there was no one around. Then I realized that the sound did not come from outside instead it was the echo of my inner self.

Report VI

Today I was so engrossed in Muraqaba that when suddenly someone tapped me on my shoulder, I was taken aback and opened my eyes. When I looked, there was no one around. Then I went back to Muraqaba. After that, every time I think of my body I felt like shivering. In the past few days, I have also noticed that every time I drink water, it tastes sugary. It seems like my sense of taste is going through some changes. Sometimes I hear whistles in my ears.

Report VII

After doing Muraqaba, I performed the pre-dawn (*fajr*) prayer. I remained focused during the entire prayers. On one occasion the idea that God is in front of me during the prayers became so strong that I felt overwhelmed by it. That state lasted for quite a while. During Muraqaba, I felt as if the *dhikr* was performed by my inner self.

Report VIII

I gained full concentration during Muraqaba and then I felt as if I were ascending into the space and have reached the higher ground. In my mind, I heard the echo so profound that it is virtually impossible to describe it. That sound made me somewhat frightened. With this feeling of fright, I saw Jerusalem where people were praying. I was staring at the Dome of the Rock. During this moment, an unseen creature whispered in my ears. I was overwhelmed by that whisper. The voice on the whisper said," staring at the Dome is not the noble deed. What is noble is to contemplate on the lives of the Prophets and Apostles, to see what hidden treasures of Divine Knowledge these noble beings held. Every member of the human race is entitled to access these treasures".

Hearing this message made me highly anxious. My heartbeat went up and I came out of the state of Muraqaba. At that time, my body was soaked due to sweating.

(Kamal)

Varood (esoteric vision)

When awareness (*idraak*) gets deeper it turns into vision and esoteric information manifests into pictorial form before the sight. This state in Sufism is called *varood*. It begins when with higher concentration drowsiness goes away and the esoteric vision gets underway. All of a sudden, any scene would come before the sight. Since consciousness is not used to seeing in this fashion, that is why mental concentration fluctuates. Memory is able to retain some part of the vision that appears before the eyes, while the rest goes into oblivion. Over time, the student gets used to this condition (state) and this process of observation continues during Muraqaba. Sometime the observation becomes so deep that the students consider themselves part of the vision. Observations become more orderly and the mind is able to comprehend what it sees.

Report IX

Compared to previous weeks, this week was great as far as my Muraqaba conditions are concerned. I was able to get deeper in my imagination and was able to focus as well. Another point to mention is that I have also been successful in maintaining focus during regular obligatory prayers. When the eyes are concentrated, at one point then the sight is stuck and becomes deeper and the esoteric eye starts seeing things. During prayers holy places come before my eyes.

In addition, I have noticed that I have pretty much overcome the inferiority complex and have since gained confidence and faith. Today all day, my mind remained focused. I have also noticed that when I am thinking about something that thing or event comes right before my eyes. Mind negated the space to such an extent that every country, every city seems to be just few steps away. Karachi, Lahore etc all of them seem so close. My mind has gone through an unbridled expansion and speed.

(Ehsan, Swat)

Report X

I see different things during Muraqaba. At the same time I feel hot and sometimes this feeling become unbearable. That is why I have short-ened the duration of my daily Muraqaba.

I saw during the Muraqaba that there is a luminous body just few steps from my body. The more my focus was enhanced, the more that body became luminous. Even the heart seems luminous. I felt that if my forehead has an eye. During the Muraqaba, I felt like if I am seeing with my forehead eye. Wherever I see, things appeared to be collection of var-ious colors. (Waqar Ahmed)

Report XI

During Muraqaba, due to enhanced concentration, I became totally unaware of my physical body and my body of aura became more promi-nent. I felt as if the universe existed inside my body and toward my lower back; the electric current was spreading to my entire body. Suddenly I felt a shock and my aura and I were separated. I saw a huge space and my aura was floating in there. From that aura a wave of light emanated through which everything in space became visible.

(M. Aslam)

Ilhaam (revelation)

In some people, the esoteric sense of hearing is activated before the activation of esoteric vision. Once it is activated, the person is able to hear voices and sounds from beyond. At first, the thoughts come in the form of voices. Eventually the consciousness of that person becomes strong enough that whenever he or she focuses, its hidden affairs and futuristic details enter the hearing faculty in the form of sounds. When this is repeated over time then the sight is activated as well. In the end, the hidden and futuristic information manifests itself in the pictorial form. This condition or state is known as *kashaf.*

In the beginning, the *kashaf* happens involuntarily. Suddenly through a thought, sound, or the image, something is revealed and later on is proven.

Example

You are sitting in your living room. Suddenly an old friend comes to your mind and hours later, either he or she comes to visit you or calls you unexpectedly. The second condition is that you hear a voice announcing the arrival of your friend or the third condition is that you actually see him or her coming way ahead of their actual arrival.

When this ability of *kashaf* progresses the person achieves the level in which outward (physical) and inward (esoteric) senses work simultaneously. The mind of the student becomes so strong that he or she observes the material and spiritual world simultaneously. When this state is achieved, the person no longer needs the closure of eyes for the Muraqaba. This particular state is exclusively involuntary. It could initiate while the person is busy walking, talking, and sitting and goes off suddenly as well. This condition may occur several times during the day or sometimes may not occur for weeks. This condition is known as *Ilhaam.*

Proof of Vahii

Qur'an (Koran) Sura aal- imran 66:

> "These events are among the news of the unseen. We do *vahii* about them to you. And you were not there when they were drawing to decide who would take care of Mary. And you were not there when they were disputing among themselves."

According to the above verse, the *vahii* comes from God. *Vahii* is that form of pure light (*nur*) that carries esoteric information. This information may be of past events or of future happenings. That is why God has informed His prophets and apostles of both the past (history) and the future. Other than that *vahii* has nothing to do with the individual's consciousness or discretion. Instead, *vahii* is in fact Divine Wisdom.

Sura Aeraaf 203:

> "And when you do not bring any *ayat* to them- they say- why did you not make it on your own? Say, I only follow what was *vahii* to me from my Lord. These are the bright signs from your Lord. They are guidance and blessing for those people who are of faith."

Vahii is further explained in Sura- shura 51-52:

> "And no human has the privilege to converse with Him (directly) unless through *vahii* or behind the Veil or else

He sends a messenger on whom He would *vahii* whatever He pleases. Verily He is of High Glory and Wise.
And just like that we sent a *vahii* toward you; Our Word
through Our Will. You knew neither what book was nor
what faith was. But We made that book a *nur*. We guide
whomever We wish among Our servants."

In these verses, all types of *vahii* are discussed. God has called *vahii*
His words. The word of God is revealed in many different ways.
Sometimes through *vahii* while at others, mysteriously. For instance,
Moses glimpsed the Divine Light (*tadjalli*). On Mount Sinai God
revealed His Divine Light in the burning bush. Moses conversed with
God. This type of *vahii* is known as the hidden or veiled one. This Divine
Light became the veil between God and Moses. So that he was not able
to see God, instead he only glimpsed the Divine Veil. Through this Veil,
he communicated with God.

In other case, *vahii* was delivered to the prophets through Archangel
Gabriel. After the end of prophethood *vahii* is no longer used. However,
its sub-types (branches) *kashaf, ilhaam* and *alqaa* (intuition) still exist.
This is what was mentioned in the above verses of the *Qur'an* (Koran)
that no human has the privilege. Here the word human is used, prophet
or apostle was not used. This suggests that even an ordinary mortal can
communicate with the Divine through the sub-type of *vahii*. Also included in these sub-types are true dreams.

In Sura Nahal of the *Qur'an* (Koran), God is said to have *vahii* a honeybee. The *vahii* of honeybee is also a part of its sub branch, which is different from the *vahii* sent to the prophets and apostles. That system
which was designated for prophets and apostles ended with the closure
of prophethood. Nevertheless, even after the prophets, God's wisdom
and His discretion and His communication with His creatures continue
through the sub-branches of *vahii*.

God is pure light (*nur*). His words are also *nur*. Although God is as
close to us as our jugular nerve, we are unable to comprehend His
Essence with our conscious (physical) senses. Which means that for us
to absorb *vahii*, which is the light (*nur*) of the Word of God, our consciousness has to be powerful or strong enough so that it can withstand
its impact. Based on these levels of consciousness, there are several
forms of *vahii*.

God's prophets are trained and taught directly by the Divine, that is
why their conciousness was strong enough to absorb the pure light (*nur*)
of *vahii* directly into their *latifa' qalbi* (generator of heart). All the generators (*latifa*) of Soul are the center points where the incoming lights
(*nur*) are stored. The generators of Heart (*latifa qalbi*) and Soul (*latifa
nafsi*) are the spheres in which all the worldly lights are kept, which

means that under normal circumstances these spheres absorb the material (physical) lights. However under unique circumstances these centers can also absorb and store the non physical light *(nur)* and the Divine light *(tadjalli)*. Their strength can be enhanced at will. Until the ability to absorb *nur* is established, no *nur* can be transferred, just as a full glass cannot hold any more water.

The lights that are transferred into consciousness from the subconscious are the cognition of the spirit *(ruh)*. This cognition performs under the influence of *nur* and *tadjalli*. In other words, the human spirit *(ruh insani)* has three usual lenses. One lens (sight) works in the material world. The second works in the realm of pure light *(nur)*. And the third one works in the realm of Divine Light *(tadjalli)*.

In all three zones of the universe, there are worlds of living creatures. In every zone the system of the Divine Names is working. The fixed quantity of these Divine Names is controlling all the systems of the universe. In every zone different quantities of the *tadjalli* are working. Based on the level of these quantities, the universal system is composed of various formulas. These formulas can be observed with the help of the lens of the Divine Light *(tadjalli)*. With the lens of the pure light *(nur)* the esoteric form of the things that are formed by these formulas can be seen. Moreover, with the material lens the outward or physical body of these things can be observed. Hence, any particular being exists simultaneously in all three zones. In other words, the universe is divided into three zones. One of the zones is visible to us all the time; however, the other two are hidden from our sight.

The zones that are hidden from the sight are the subconscious. The sight of the spirit *(ruh)* that functions in the subconscious and works in multiple layers of the spirit continuously sends information to the consciousness. Every layer of the spirit is in constant motion by the Divine Will. Hence information of every movement is being transferred from the subconscious. This is what is known as the news of the hidden.

The news that comes from the layer of Divine light *(tadjalli)* to the consciousness is *vahii*. Cognition in the sphere of Divine Light enables the consciousness to observe the descending state of the universe. God has given the spirit His creative knowledge. When the Divine light goes through the layers of the spirit then the cognition of the spirit transforms it into a creative form. This form goes through pure light *(nur)* and lights and then eventually takes it physical form and comes before the eye.

When the speed of the subconscious and consciousness becomes even (parallel) then all three layers of the spirit are activated simultaneously and their mutual distance disappears. The descending Divine Light then falls directly into the consciousness. In this condition the consciousness of the Divine Light becomes dominant. Divine Cognition becomes dominant and the creature cognition becomes dormant (submissive).

Among the prophets of God the most subtle of Divine Light works. They are able to recognize the Divine Wisdom through their own Spirit. The subtle senses of the Spirit take them over and even in the physical world they live with the senses of the Spirit.

The Divine light is not God but the reflection of His Essence. The Divine light is His Veil (*hijab e'lahi*). No one can glimpse God beyond His Divine Veil nor can any of His creatures access Him without it.

The universe is the creation of God. The vision of the spirit sees and recognizes every being in its creative form. For unless a being becomes a created figure, it remains unrecognized and unnamed.

Spirit (*ruh*) is the Divine Will (*amr*). Human Spirit spreads God' Will into the universe. First, the Spirit transforms itself into the ultra-pure-light (*tadjalli*) of the Divine Will. Just as when software is downloaded into the computer, its hardware converts the cryptic script into a creative picture (or design) and displays it into the monitor. The cryptic script of the software is nothing but numbers or alphabets (formulas). That formula or language then is read by the hardware, which in turn displays the creative graphics. In the same manner, a whole being in the complete shape and form is recognized.

The *tadjalli* sphere of the Spirit in turn absorbs the ultra-pure-light (*tadjalli*) which was sent by God into the spirit (*ruh*). These ultra-pure-lights are of the fixed quantities of the Divine Wisdom. Each quantity is one of the formulas of the universe. This formula is what is displayed to the Spirit. In other words, the inner realm of the creation comes forward. In it lie the lights of the Divine Names (*isma e'lahiya*) and the details of their movements and systems. Then in the sphere of the ordinary lights, the physical form of the being is manifested. This body performs its functions and motions based on the program that was downloaded in it.

The reality of *vahii* is that in the consciousness those ultra-pure-lights descend that are send by God to the spirit (*ruh*). The spirit then converts these ultra-pure-lights into consciousness. And consciousness through cognition puts meanings into these ultra-pure-lights. At the time of the descent of *vahii* the speed of consciousness becomes parallel to the speed of subconscious. That is why the words of *vahii* do not carry the lights of worldly thoughts.

Although after the closure of prophethood the system of *vahii* was terminated, the knowledge brought in by the prophets still exists in this world. The Divine Word, in the form of Holy Scriptures are with us. Whenever a person imitates the lifestyles of the prophets by being righteous, the lights of this knowledge start filling in his Spirit.

By sending this *vahii* to His prophets, God activated (awakened) their consciousness to a point where they were able to recognize the movements of their spirit. Moreover, through their own Self (*inner*) they were able to recognize (*Gnosis*) the Attributes of God.

Whoever follows the path of prophets is able to gain the perspective of the prophets and through their medium, is able to acquire the Divine Knowledge, through which they become aware of the cosmic system.

Kashaf

Report XII

When I closed my eyes for Muraqaba, suddenly glitters of light started appearing and I began to watch various things. I heard the voices of many close relatives. Voices were so clear that on one occasion I ended up talking to someone during Muraqaba. Towards the end of Muraqaba when I saw myself leaving my own body and ascending towards the roof, I panicked and opened my eyes and started staring at the roof where I saw something was moving upwards.

I saw the tomb of the Prophet during Muraqaba and then saw a chain of mountains. In its valley, there was a beautiful garden. Everywhere I saw greenery. It was a magnificent view. One day, I became so engrossed during Muraqaba that I became unaware of the surroundings. When for a moment my mind got distracted, even the breathing moments seem to be interrupting. When a thought of an old friend came to my mind it appeared as if he were standing there and I was watching him clearly.

One day during Muraqaba my mind started thinking about some relatives. Suddenly I started hearing people talking. I could hear their conversation very clearly. The next day when I asked them about the conversation they confirmed that those were the things they were talking about.

Report XIII

When I was praying the *isha* prayer I felt as if the prophet Muhammad were leading the prayers. I was standing right behind him. On my right side were Qalander Baba (founder of the Azeemia order) and on my left was Baba Ji (Author). Dignitaries from other religions were there too. All the time I kept seeing, the lights from Prophet Muhammad emitting and falling on me. I could see him (Prophet) very clearly in the midst of those illuminating lights though his back was towards me. He was dressed in Arabic attire. His face was glowing and illuminating. There was a circle of pure light surrounding him. I was right behind him and that is why his lights were directly shining on me.

My entire attention was on him. That is why I was not able to see the faces of those people who were there.

Report XIV

I saw myself as if made of *tadjalli*. My body was very bright and I was sitting at a place where there was nothing but lights. In this luminary place I was sitting in a Muraqaba posture. I was still and my open eyes were fixed at the space in front of me. My mind was blank just like a slate. Suddenly I saw a fast moving light come and enter my forehead.

(Saeeda Khatoon, Manchester).

Report XV

At 8:15 pm I was sitting at my living room. Suddenly a milky circle of one and a half cubic feet emerged in the front wall. It kept moving from one end to the other. The room was lit by mercury lights (tube lights) but the lights emitting from that circle were brighter. This continued for about 10 minutes. Suddenly a new figure emerged which was even brighter than the previous one. That figure lasted for about 5-6 minutes. Meanwhile, I kept on staring at those figures. I was not aware of the surroundings. When these luminary figures finally left, I felt as if my brain had an electric shock. At that moment, a thought came to my mind that that figure was in fact Qalander Baba. There was a similarity between his facial expression and that figure. I started sobbing immediately. I could not describe how I felt at that moment. My heartbeat went so high that I was afraid my heart would pop out of my month.

(Rehana)

Report XVI

Suddenly I felt as if there were a body coming out of my own body and then that body took off from the window towards the sky. The body was attired in a white luminary dress. The whole space had a white cloudy stuff in it. That luminary body covered seven different ways as it was ascending. The scene was magnificent, there was white lights everywhere.. That body seemed a little worried at one point. Then it lifted is face upward and a voice was heard "God will help you". When my spiritual body heard this voice, my physical body started shaking. Heartbeat went up. Then I heard "*Al-Lahu Akbar*" (God is greatest) and then I bowed and prostrated. Wished I could spend my whole life in that posture. Then I saw several angels in two rows facing each other. There was a 5-6 foot distance between the rows. My spiritual body came in between then. The moment I tried to look up, I started trembling.

Report XVII

Right after I closed my eyes to begin Muraqaba I felt as if I came out of my physical body and was inside the tomb of Prophet Muhammad.

Right away, I started reciting *durud* in my heart. I felt as if a cooler light were falling on me from the holy fence of the tomb. Then I saw myself inside the Kaaba in Mecca. Moments later the Kaaba started ascending towards the sky. I saw different types of people during the journey. Some of them I knew. Eventually we reached a dead end. Here I saw row after row of angels. Then I saw myself in my room and felt that my being was spread throughout the entire room. I ended the Muraqaba at this point.

On another day during Muraqaba I saw a line of light traveling from the west to the south. I stopped at my house. At that point, I felt as if that light were in fact me. When I tried to focus then all the events of my life, from birth to present day were displayed like a movie. In them there were happy moments, sad ones, good, bad, everything was there. When I focused more, some future events were displayed as well. I was able to comprehend some of them while others were not clear. Then I saw that spiritual body among stars in the sky. But I was not able to keep my focus on that and I ended the Muraqbah.

(Ali Asghar, Saltcoats UK).

Report XVIII

During Muraqaba I saw *Murshid Kareem* (Author) with me. He then said, "Let's go see the skies." We then started ascending. Our bodies were floating like birds. We then entered the skies. We went through clouds of very bright lights which lead to a very clear space. Below there are different cities. Many people were seen working in their field. It was lush green. Big clean rivers were running as well. On the banks of the river, people had crops of different vegetables, fruits, and stuff. We saw all that in one blink of an eye and resumed our upward flight. We entered the clouds of light again and later moved on to another clear space, which had valleys and towns all over the place. We then moved on to another clear space after going through other clouds of light. As we sent through the clouds it felt as if this were the border of the heavens.

I then asked *Murshid Kareem* (author) that I thought that the border between two skies would be of steel or other harder substance which would make it impossible to penetrate. Instead, all I see is lights after lights, which can be penetrated very easily. There is no hurdle here. *Baba Ji* (author) replied, "The sky is the limit of human sight. When consciousness enters the field of subconscious, its sight gradually increases, and man's inner sight beholds the realm of subconscious (*a'lam al-ghayb*). To behold the realm of the hidden, there is no restriction imposed by God. However, on every level of the sky, the worlds that exist are under the influence of different lights of Divine Attributes. The reason why the consciousness is unable to see beyond the sky is that it remains ignorant of the Laws of Lights of Divine Names (*isma e'lahiya*).

But when someone gains the knowledge of the Laws of the Divine Names, he or she then can enter the realm of subconscious at will and consciously. They then can observe the realm of the hidden (*a'lam al-ghayb*) without any hurdle with their 'inner' vision.

Every level of sky is made of those lights of Divine Names that are responsible for its creation. Due to the concentration of lights of Divine Names at the border of the sky, our regular vision is unable to see anything beyond that.

However, when one contemplates the Divine Essence and Attributes, the lights of the Divine Names start penetrating their being. These Divine Lights introduce themselves to consciousness and it becomes aware of their presence. Its awareness is in fact its vision. In this world the amount of absorption of light depends on how far the person is knowledgeable of the Divine Names. After his death his station in the hereafter (*aeraaf*) depends on it. This means that after death the person lives with his outward senses and vision in the hereafter.

I was really glad when I heard this explanation from *Baba Ji* (author). Then I asked him if it was necessary to acquire knowledge of Divine Names in this world in order to gain access to these realms.

He said, "Merely acquiring knowledge and becoming aware of something is not enough. Unless and until the characteristics of the Divine Names are performed in the individual, he or she would not be able to have access to this realm upon his or her death. That is why God has created seven skies so that the individual be able to learn the science of each and every light of Divine Names working in each level of sky and slowly their consciousness able to absorb these lights. Every sky is the level of growth of consciousness. Each sky shows the different speed of consciousness. This means that the senses that exist in the consciousness, functions in the corresponding speed that exists in these realms. When the individual speed of senses becomes parallel to that of the speed of the senses of those who live in these realms, only then the individual is finally able to gain access to these realms and journeys through it and acquires their knowledge". The realm where after death the spirit of the deceased is transferred is called the realm of *aeraaf*.

In the dream I see that the *Baba Ji* (author) hand is on the top of my head like an umbrella. From his fingers the lights are being transferred to my brain because of which my brain becomes extremely bright and I started to fly in the space like a bird. Even during the flight, I saw his hand on top of my head. During the flight I kept the *dhikr* and offered thanks and praise to God Almighty. At the same time, I kept looking below to see where I was flying. I saw the land of *aeraaf* below. I then decided to visit it. I landed on its soil and started walking around to see things. It was a very beautiful city. There were garden lakes everywhere.

The weather was nice. I kept praising and thanking the Lord. During that time, I entered an area where there were small houses and even with this nice weather and greenery, every one was staying inside. My vision went inside and I saw people were sitting heads down and very depressed. As if they had no energy to lift their heads and see the beauty outside in order to uplift their spirit.

I felt as if they were engrossed in the memory of the world that they had left behind. A thought came to my mind that Allah did not stop them from enjoying the good weather and scenery; they had imposed the imprisonment on themselves. If they take just two steps to come outside then the open air would wash away all their agonies and despair and they would become happy and content. Some of them looked familiar. I convinced them to leave the place and come outside.

Then after that, I came across a very modern housing area. Big castles like homes and their designs resemble geometric figures. They were colored with very light paints and looked fabulous. Then I saw someone whom I had known. He had died few weeks ago. He was very glad to see me and then he said,   "Auntie! You are here. How come?"

He was wearing a tailored suit. I was glad to see him too. I said to him that I went to the other end of *aeraaf* where instead of happiness all I saw was misery. It is a good thing that I see you. He then said let's go and see things. First, he said he was going to take me to his home. We sat in the car. He told me that he had designed the car himself. That car resembled a flying saucer. Very beautiful, however there was no steering wheel, no gear, nothing in it except a few buttons. I then asked him how it was going to run.

He said, "Auntie! Wherever you want to go, simply think about it and this car will take you there. And it was true. He thought about a place and then the car started moving at high speed and stopped at a huge white palace. Its design was also based on the geometric figures but looked very elegant. He showed me his home, his cars, everything, was very advanced. He said that the mental speed of the people here was far greater than those of Earth. However, even here there were towns where people were living primitively. I then felt that those people who remain ignorant of God's Knowledge willingly are leading an even more morose living here. Because the speed of this world was at least 10,000 times faster then our world (Earth), nothing can increase the speed of mind but knowledge and the faster the mind gets, the more practical the individual becomes. Then in this fast-paced society every one has to catch up in order to fit in. Otherwise they become isolated and depressed and find no one but themselves for pity. After watching all this, I thanked God for letting me acquire all these branches of knowledge.

Mrs. Abdul Hafeez Butt, England

16
Spiritual Journey

In the Spirits of humans there exists a light, which as far as its boundary is concerned, is limitless. If we were to attempt to put a boundary on it then virtually the entire universe has be included as well. This particular light covers every piece of existence. No thought, whim or imagination can escape from it. In this circle of light any event that has already happened or is in the process of happening or is going to happen, everything is right across the vision of the Man.

One of the rays of this light is vision. This ray travels from the far corners of the universe. In other words, the entire universe is a circle and this light is a lamp. The rays of this lamp are vision. Wherever this ray falls, it beholds the surroundings near and far. The rays of the lamp have different levels. Sometimes the rays that fall vary from being very low, to intense and very intense.

Objects on which very low ray falls create a whim in our mind about those things. A whim is actually the most subtle thought, which can only be felt in the depth of perception.

Objects on which a low ray falls create a thought in our mind about those things. Objects on which an intense ray falls cause imagination of those things to appear in our mind. And when a very intense ray falls then our vision reaches it and beholds it.

Anything that remains in the stages of whim, thought, or imagination remains unclear for the human vision and it is unable to comprehend its details. But when the circle of vision keeps increasing then those things become visible which the vision is already familiar with, such as whim, thought and imagination.

When vision reaches the rays, whether very low or very intense, it is called *shahood*. It is an ability that brings even the very low beam of rays into the vision so that those objects that were at this point merely whims could now be seen as holding form and figure, color and shape.

Shahood is that power of the Spirit that brings the whim, thought or imagination towards the vision and downloads its details into it. In it, the electrical system of the Spirit intensifies and the senses are able to store more and more lights, to a point where the unseen (*al-ghayb*) features becomes visible. This stage is the first step of *shahood*. In this stage all functions are related to vision, meaning the person with *shahood* (*sahib shahood*) witnesses the affairs of the unseen, literally.

After the vision, the second stage of *shahood* pertains to hearing. In this stage, thought of any living being (human or otherwise) reaches the hearing of the person with *shahood* (*sahib shahood*) in the form of sound.

The third and fourth stages of *shahood* deals with the ability of the person with *shahood* (*sahib shahood*) of touching and smelling things even if the distance is in the thousands of years.

A companion of the Prophet Muhammad once told him. "O Prophet of God, I used to see angels walking all over the sky" (during his night vigils, which he later discontinued).

Prophet Muhammad replied, "If you had kept the night vigils, you would have been able to shake hands with angels as well."

In the event above that occurred in the time of Prophet Muhammad the stages of *shahood* are mentioned. Seeing angels has to do with spiritual vision and shaking hands points to the ability of touch, that are awakened after the vision and hearing.

Among the stages of *shahood,* one of its states is when the physical and spiritual transpires summed up into one point and the body becomes obedient (submissive) to the spirit.

There are many anecdotes available from the life of Spiritual Masters that refer to this. For example one of the close acquaintances of Sufi Master Shaykh Maroof Karkhi, saw a mark on the body of the master, which was not there a day before and inquired him about that.

Shaykh Maroof Karkhi replied, "last night during the evening prayers my focus went towards the Kaaba. And after circling when I went near the fountain of *zam-zam,* I slipped and fell, I got this mark from that."

A similar incident happened to me [the author]. One day I saw an injury on the body of my Spiritual Master Qalander Baba Awliya (1896-1979) and inquired about it. He replied that in the previous night during Muraqaba he was flying between two hills and his body got hit by one of the hills during that spiritual flight.

When the conditions of *shahood* are fully developed then the spiritual student travels the unseen realm as if he were living in it. He travels, eats, drinks, and engages in all those works that can be labeled as his spiritual pastimes (hobby). This condition is only achieved when along with practicing Muraqaba the student is full detached from worldly affairs. He becomes free of any boundaries of Time and Space. He ventures from the beginning of Time to the end of it, as well.

When the Point of Essence (*nuqta dhat*) in man becomes fully knowledgeable about the activities of Muraqaba then it expands to such an extent then he is able to access Time from its beginning to the end and is able to use his new-found spiritual powers at will. He is able to witness events that occurred thousands of years ago or are going to occur thousands of years from today. From the beginning to the end of time, whatever existed before or will happen exists at this moment.

In his book *Loh-o-Qalam* (Urdu, Al-Kitab Publications) Qalander Baba Awliya wrote, "when the spiritual journey of the Gnostic (*arif*) begins, he never enters the universe from an outward source; instead through his inner Point of Essence (*nuqta dhat*). This point is where the Unity of Being (*wahdat ul wajud*) begins. When the Gnostic lets his vision observe that point, then an opening of light occurs. Through that door of light, he enters a highway through which he goes to any dimension in the entire cosmic systems, stays in various satellites and stars and comes across as many creatures in these places. He is then able to get acquainted with the outward and the inward side of existence. Later on he becomes aware of the realities and the truth of the universe. The mysteries of creation open up to him. He then becomes aware of the Divine Laws of Nature. He then gets acquainted with his own Soul. Then his cognition accepts spiritual ways. He gets awareness of the Divine Light and Divine Attributes.

He then fully understands that when God commanded *kun* (to be) how the Universe came into being and how stage after stage of being is still evolving. He understands that he, too, is part of that being.

It must be noted that the above-mentioned journey does not open up in the outward dimension. Its mark exists in the depth of the center of the heart. No one should mistakenly think that *that* realm is merely an unreal world of thoughts and imagination. On the contrary, all those realities that exist as forms and figures exist in this world as well."

Qalander Baba Awliya further explains the details of *shahood*: "The spiritual student gets acquainted with angels and becomes aware of things hidden in his own reality. He recognizes those qualities that he possesses. The realities of the world are revealed on him. He sees with his own eyes the kinds of light that are a part of the structure of this universe and what other pure lights (*nur*) are controlling those lights. Then he gets awareness of the Divine Light (*tadjalli*) that is the source of all those pure lights (*nur*).

17
Fatah (Exploration)

The highest level of *shahood* is known as *fatah* (exploration). This happens when someone gains excellence in *shahood* to a point where while witnessing the unseen he is unable to close his eyes owing to the mounting pressure; they are compelled to remain open. When that happens then *sayr* (journey), *shahood* and other spiritual experiences are witnessed with open eyes. During this stage, the student witnesses the period between the creation and the end-time with his own eyes while performing normal daily routines of his life. From the far corners of the universe, he sees creation in progress, the birth of numerous galaxies and their stars, their chronological evolution and their eventual demise as well.

A mere second of *fatah* sometimes may be an encircling of the period between creation to the end time. Experts of Astronomy claim that it takes more or less four years for any light, that is from any system other than our own solar system, to reach us. According to them, there are even some stars whose light reaches us in thousands of years. This means the stars that we look at night are the figure that existed thousands of years ago. We are then bound to recognize the fact that the present moment is a thousand years old moment. A point to ponder is that between these two moments, which are *in fact* one, thousands of years elapse. Where do those thousand of years go?

This suggests that these thousands of years are nothing but an angle of perception. This has divided this single moment into thousands and thousands of years. Just as this angle of perception sees the thousands of years in the present moment, it could as well see the future thousands of years in the present moment. Therefore, the period from the creation to the end is a single moment that has been divided by the angle of perception into the various stages between the beginning and the end of time.

This division is what we know as Space (*makaan*), meaning the entire period between the creation and the end is Space (*makaan*) and all the incidents that this universe has seen are confined in the divisions of that single moment. It is the grace of the perception that has given that moment the appearance of the beginning to the end.

The perception that we are used to could never be able to see the length of that single moment. The perception that could is mentioned in the *Sura* Qadar of *Qur'an* (Koran):

"And We have revealed this during the night of power. And what dost thou sense what night of power is? That night of power is better than thousands of months. Angels and the Holy Spirit descend on that night by the Will of their Lord to do the work. That night is all peace till dawn."

The aforesaid night of power is that perception that reveals the affairs of the period between creation and the end-time. This perception is thirty thousand times or even greater than the normal perception because one night was compared with thousand of months. With the help of this perception man is able to get acquainted with the spirits and angels and witness the mysteries of creation.

The following is an excerpt from the author's book *Jannat Ki Sayr* (Urdu, Al-Kitab Publications) in which he is relating an incident from the early days of his spiritual life.

I was returning home from the city market in a bus. It was so crowded that it seemed like passengers were loaded like a cargo. Besides exhaust fumes and heat, the smell of passengers sweating was all over the bus. Every time when the bus would restart after the stops, the air filtering through the sweats of passengers would make my brain explode.

A few passengers were wearing perfumes while others had the hair creams that smelled like a stinking drug. This mixture of bad and good smells was giving me a headache and I felt like I was being suffocated. When this happened suddenly a thought crossed my mind, why there is so much odor in a man?

My mind was so focused on that thought that my eyes became a little mushy. Then I saw a circle. There were six more circles on top of that. Each circle was made of a different color. Some were blue while others were green, red, or black and one was transparent. My I concentrated on those circles. Suddenly they turned into six more circles *(chakra)* and suddenly I became aware that every creation exists under these six circles *(chakra)*.

When I paid more attention to it the space between them started to increase. First circle *(chakra)* was seen in the middle of the head, second one at the forehead, third under the neck, fourth one in the middle of the chest, fifth one at the heart and the sixth one at the navel.

The circle *(chakra)* at the navel was dark and dingy. I was a bit surprised to find that in the middle of all those bright circle *(chakra)*s there existed this dark, polluted and dingy circle *(chakra)* but why? I felt as if my mind had already left my body. The body of bones and flesh felt like an empty envelope. I was no longer aware that I was traveling in a bus. I saw that on every man's shoulders there were two angels. They were writing something, however, the way they were writing was not the way we write in our world. They had no pen, nor tablet on which to write. The angel's' mind would take notice of something and that would appear in the form of a film. The forms and figures of the film would show if the mind of one of them was engaged in thoughts of greed while someone else is busy thinking about jealousy and other negative thoughts. A third person is bent on murdering someone. This person left his home with this plan. One of the angels quickly inspired him that murdering someone is a big sin and the punishment for this crime is execution. Nevertheless, this person would ignore this inspired message and kept on going according to his plan.

When the inspiration failed, the other angel took notice of it and recorded that person's plan to commit murder and the entire episode appeared on that film including his rejection of the inspiration. This person went ahead and stabbed to death another human being just like him. The second angel recorded the entire incident.

After committing the murder, that person's conscience became uneasy. His mind was now burdened with an enormous guilt and the realization that he will eventually have to pay for this crime. That guilt itself became an image in the recording.

These three men acted on their will and the way they had planned the outcome in their mind and acted on their schemes, every action and every movement became an image that was recorded by the angels. On the other hand, there was another person who left his home for prayers in the mosque. After entering the mosque he with honest heart prostrated himself before God. God loves honesty.

Because of God's approval of honesty, he became eligible for Divine Mercy *(rahma)* and rewards. Even though he did not know whether his prayers were approved, because his intentions were pure, after performing the prayers his conscience became content and he felt peace and serenity. The station of peace and serenity is heaven. After becoming content, his consciousness became aware that his final station is heaven.

The moment focus shifted to heaven, the entire heaven with its trees, fruits, creatures, lakes of honey, the well of *kauthar*, they all came into my vision. When consciousness was able to witness all that, then the angel turned his focus on the film and this entire episode was recorded in his film as well.

On the other hand, there was another man who also left his home for prayer. His mind is filled with filth and hatred for God's creatures. Injustice is his hobby. Cruelty, insensitivity, and violence are his favorite actions. He entered the mosque and prayed for a while; however, his conscience is not satisfied. This unsatisfactory condition of conscience can be labeled nothing but the condition of hell. This person finished his prayers but his conscience was not content. The angel in his film also recorded this state.

The Angels then told me:

"There are two different characters in front of you. One of the characters ignored the angelic inspiration and instead followed his own carnal impulses and went ahead and killed his fellow human being. One of the other persons performed an action which otherwise seems like a nice deed but his intentions were not honest. He was deceiving himself. The second group is the one whose intentions are honest, their minds are pure and clean, and they do respect the Divine laws. Now we are going to give you the accounts of the daily life of one person from each group.

"The one committed the murder. Whenever he gets time off from the grind of daily busy life is afflicted with enormous guilt. His heart gets uneasy and his mind gets worried and confused and he finally sinks into depression. Now the images on the film made by the angels get deeper as the things get worse by the will of that person. The bright circle *(chakra)* inside that person gets dim and that cloud finally settles on the circle *(chakra)* that is at the navel. At the circle *(chakra)*, the lights are absorbed by the darkness. When someone gets in this state then darkness and dinginess become a smelly wound. That smell becomes part of that person's blood. This stage gets worse to a point when the other circle *(chakra)* get out of touch with that person."

I was absorbed listening to the sermon of the angel when I heard a huge sound. It sounded like ringing bells. When I paid attention to this sweet melody, my hearing was struck by a voice saying:

"God has sealed their hearts, their ears and their sight with a heavy curtain, for these disobedient the punishment is everlasting damnation. "

The moment I heard this voice my heart became so fearful that I started trembling. I felt as if all the pores in my body had opened. I was shocked and started crying. I was weeping so strongly that I ended up having hiccoughs. People who saw thought that I was some crazy person. Some were even sarcastic and made fun of me. How unfortunate it was that not a single person expressed any sympathy towards me. I then left the bus and started walking towards my home.

When I got home it was dark, but I was so morose from the experience that I went straight to bed. I was really hurting. It felt like someone had nailed my heart. Suddenly my focus turned towards the mercifulness and kindness of the Prophet Muhammad. I saw those two angels were still present and trying to comfort me. The angel, who was making the film of good deeds, started to open his film right in front of me and that film turned into a screen.

Glory to God! That same circle *(chakra)* at navel which was dark and smelly turned into a bright circle *(chakra)* right in front of my eyes. It was so bright that the brightness of the sun seemed like a lamp in comparison. That filth and sadness imposed on my mind was washed away in an instant.

That person who had offered his prayers with purity and had in his heart respect for the laws created by God was also present. The rays from the bright circle *(chakra)* inside that man were revolving like the rays from the sun. It was placid almost like a still ocean. The bright and shiny heart was festive and intoxicated with ecstasy and in this joyous occasion that person was strolling in the valley of Paradise. The scenery of paradise is beyond words. The palaces were so great that no one in this world could even imagine the artistic beauty of their architecture. In the middle of the palace of diamonds and pearls I saw that same man resting. For his service there were *hoorins* and different types of birds were busy singing as if they were singing his praise. The pools were made of rare pearls and precious stones whose beauty far exceeds any worldly gems.

There is a higher station in heaven which is reserved for people who pray to God with purity and honesty. Their hearts are filled with the desire to serve God's creatures. Their hearts are seekers of Truth and they respect other human beings as an offspring of Adam and Eve. They feel others' pain as their own and try their best to relieve them of their misery. By beholding that serene world, I, myself became peaceful. I surrendered my intelligence and my hearing seemed to be sinking. The sight that sees the world seemed like a fake and my eyes became watery. However, these were not the tears of sadness and fear but were of thankfulness. After seeing me happy the angels became happy as well and then they inquired of me, "Do you know whose station is this?"

"This is the station of those who followed the path of God's prophets with honesty and these are those whom the God has called His friend (*wali*). Verily God's friends have neither fear nor are they accustomed to sadness."

These angels were *kramin katibeen.*

18
Classification of Muraqaba

Experts of Muraqaba have taught their students various methods of performing Muraqaba. These different Muraqabas work like a class or grade for the spiritual development of the students; so their progress would evolve gradually. When a student gains excellence in any one of the types of Muraqaba, they are then promoted to the next higher level.

These different levels and their goals are based on the types of imagination that a student has to focus on during the Muraqaba. For instance, the Muraqaba of *kashaf ul qaboor* (vision of the grave) is to reveal the life after death to the student. To strengthen their aura, the student practice Muraqaba of different colors of light and to observe the pure light, they perform Muraqaba of *nur*.

Similarly, to transfer the mental aptitude and knowledge of the teacher to the student they practice the Muraqaba of imagining the teacher *(tassawar shaykh)*. In short, based on the quality, aptitude and need of the students, they practice different kinds of Muraqaba. Only an experienced, all-round teacher who has gone through the different levels of practice and has thorough knowledge of the science of Muraqaba can determine the specific Muraqaba for the student.

There are many kinds of Muraqaba based on types of imagination and methods. That is why we are going to shed some lights on the two major types of Muraqabas; the rest are the subbranches of these Muraqabas.

Along with explaining these Muraqabas, a practical program is also there so anyone could follow the instructions and get general and specific benefits from it.

Some programs for the Muraqabas are for special purposes. For instance, Muraqaba to observe life after death (*kashaf ul qaboor*), Muraqaba of voice of cosmos (*haatif ghaybi*), Muraqaba for mental peace and so on and so forth. These specialized Muraqaba can awaken any unique and hidden ability of the student so as to get specific benefit from it. While other Muraqabas work to activate the hidden senses of the student, these Muraqaba activate the so-called third eye by using specialized methods.

The program is for an average individual and the goal is not to build any pressure on the mind of the student. In case of a lack of physical presence of the teacher, the institute recommends that students send monthly journal report of their meditative visions and other experiences that they may face, so whenever necessary, they can receive guidance.

The following is the goal of the program:

1. To improve the working of the brain and mind
2. To improve the special faculties of the mind, that is, memory, creativity, imagination and its speed.
3. To awake the hidden abilities of telepathy, *kashaf.*
4. To improve cognitive and intuitive abilities.
5. To activate the spiritual sight or the third eye of the student.

Before starting to work on any of the programs, it is important to be mindful of the following:

1. Practice Muraqaba at the same time for about 15-20 minutes daily. Do not lose heart if the progress is not up to your expectation. The progress and benefits depend on the interest and the consistency of the student. Some students move slowly and their progress remains moderate, while others progress rapidly in the beginning and then later they slow. Some do not progress at all at first but later they catch up fast. In short depending on the temperament, progress rate could vary. Principally what slowly becomes part of your nature will stay more firmly.
2. Enthusiasm and great interest do not mean the student should change or alter the program on their own. Limit your enthusiasm to following and practicing the prescribed Muraqaba and other exercises (that is, respiratory exercise) with full attention and focus.

Practical Program

When we see someone performing Muraqaba, it seems as if that person is simply sitting in one posture with his eyes closed. That refers to the physical side of it as how to sit and how the surroundings should be. The real aspect of Muraqaba is its mental side. As the topic suggests, we are going to discuss the practical sides of Muraqaba. Practical side refers to a general know-how and what others things need to be taken care of.

To perform Muraqaba, you would first close your eyes and then free your mind of all the incoming thoughts. Then focus on a single idea or imagination in a way that you are no longer attached to or interested in any other thoughts or ideas. The two main parts of Muraqaba are emptiness of the mind and the idea of the imagination. Emptiness of the mind means you should not pay any attention to other thought or willingly think about anything. This is what thoughtlessness is.

You can perform Muraqaba in different ways; here we are going to shed some light on the other details.

Styles of Posture

Make the surroundings and the place to sit for Muraqaba as comfortable and serene as possible, to avoid tension in the nerves and physical fatigue. Based on your physique and natural tendencies, you can adopt any of the following sitting styles.

Cross-legged Position

Either sitting on the floor or on a cushion, double the left leg and put in on top of the right thigh. The back and neck should remain straight so it should not bend or get tense. In this position, place both hands on the knees or in the middle.

Sitting Straight Position

If you feel uncomfortable with the above posture then sit the way Muslims sit during prayers. Even in this position, be careful not to bend the back or to make it too rigid. Again, sit comfortably.

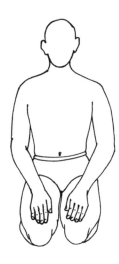

Other Styles:

One of the other styles is to sit on hips, then fold the legs upward so the knees would touch the chest, and then fold the hands around them as if embracing them. In this position, the upper body slightly leans forward. Best point about this position is that you can perform a long Muraqaba without getting tired.

You can do Muraqaba in a chair; however, keep the back straight and to avoid drowsiness do not let the body lean backward on the chair. In this position, you can perform Muraqaba on a sofa, ottoman, or in a bed. You can also perform

Muraqaba by lying down. However, we recommend avoiding this position as it leads to sleep and therefore its purpose remains unachievable. You can also do Muraqaba standing and there are some imaginations (*tassawar*) that require focusing during walking. Those Muraqabas are the exceptions; otherwise you can perform most of them in a siting position.

In a sitting position, it is a lot easier for an individual to gain focus.

Timing and Place

The more serene and peaceful the environment is going to be, the easier it will be to concentrate and achieve focus during the Muraqaba. Perform Muraqaba in a place that is neither too warm nor too cold to feel the chills. The fewer things around the lighter the mind would be. The place should have access to air as much as possible. Also the darker the better. Turn off the lights before, during and a few minutes after the Muraqaba. Let the darkness stay for awhile. If the light is pouring in from outside then use a curtain or anything else that would block it from entering the room, but keep in mind not to obstruct the flow of oxygen.

We do not recommend Muraqaba lying down in a bed as it leads to drowsiness. It is better to perform it in a sitting position either on the floor, in a chair, or on an ottoman style sofa. Attire yourself in loose clothing.

The four best periods for doing Muraqaba are:

1. before dawn
2. during early afternoon
3. late evening around an hour before sunset
4. after midnight

During these periods Nature goes through stillness and so do human senses and that is why doing Muraqaba during these times is more productive than the others. All these times have some specific benefits; however, the period between sundown and sunrise is better than the others because during nighttime those senses on which the unseen realm unfolds are more active.

Our world is moving in two ways, first in its own axis and second in its orbit. After reaching the zenith, the speed of orbiting starts slowing. Around a couple of hours before sundown, the speed slows down to a point where senses start feeling the pressure. Human and animal senses begin converting from the diurnal senses to the nocturnal senses. Every sensible person could tell you that during these hours we enter a state in which we feel tired or exhausted. This condition is the beginning of subconscious impulses on the consciousness. After midnight, the nocturnal senses get stronger and that is why it is the best period for Muraqaba.

Subconscious senses remain dominant until sunrise. That is why doing Muraqaba before sunrise is more helpful than during the daylight hours. One of the benefits of performing Muraqaba before sunrise is the overnight sleep gets rid of all the fatigue and tension of the day and therefore the person remained focused during Muraqaba. Even after waking up the subconscious senses remain active; therefore, the brain easily absorbs the effects of Muraqaba.

For many people Muraqaba around midnight may not be suitable because of job and business engagements. They are so tired that right around the time they begin the Muraqaba they fall asleep. For these people early morning Muraqaba would be the best.

The duration of the Muraqaba depends on the mental state and the concentration level of that person. The duration of the Muraqaba can be from 15 minutes to a couple of hours. Sometimes the time passes so swiftly that after finishing the Muraqaba when one looks at the watch, it is way past the intended time. While on other occasions, the person's eyes open before the scheduled time with no desire to continue. However, keep the duration of the Muraqaba to an average 20 to 45 minutes.

You should fully utilize the time reserved for Muraqaba. Perform Muraqaba peacefully with ease. Prepare yourself for the heightened mental focus the way we prepare ourselves before starting to read a book. Just as for book reading we make the environment peaceful and quiet, so make the surroundings for Muraqaba also noise-free and serene so you can achieve maximum concentration. Right before beginning the Muraqaba let the mind be free of any thoughts and be peaceful. To achieve that state words can used as well ...for example:

Say to yourself...everything is still and quiet and this stillness and serenity is entering inside me.

Say these phrases in a low voice to feel its effects. Begin Muraqaba only when your body, mind and respiration are in harmony.

Material Help

The purpose of Muraqaba is to activate the esoteric vision within us. This can only be achieved by reducing or suspending the movements of eyeballs as much as possible. The less the eyeballs move the quicker it is to activate the esoteric vision. Keeping this rule in mind, the experts of Muraqaba recommend having a band or small towel wrapped around the eyes. The darker the color the better, black is usually the color of choice. When placing the towel around the eyes make sure to secure the eyeballs with it. This grip should be neither too light nor so tight that it would cause pain in the eyes. The point is to make eyeballs feel some pressure during the Muraqaba. With enough pressure, you can control the movement of the eyeballs. During this suspended state, the esoteric vision, which we can call the spiritual eyes, becomes functional.

To protect hearing from outside noises and to focus on the inner voices, experts recommend placing a soaked cotton ball, sprinkled with black pepper powder in the ears during the Muraqaba. Black pepper is a natural sound absorber, which also helps bring the inner voice up to the hearing level.

The added advantages of having a towel wrapped around the head to control the eyes and of the cotton balls are to reduce the environmental influences. However it is not a mandatory requirement; you can perform Muraqaba without the help of the above. When you are ready with the recommended help, you should then sit in a comfortable position and after closing the eye for a few moments, let the mind be free of any thoughts. Then move the focus to the central thought of Muraqaba and then begin your practice.

Imagination

Many people are not sure what imagination or visualization is. Usually they assume that imagination suggests making picture in our head about the given subject. For example in the Muraqaba of *tassawar shaykh* (visualizing the Sufi Master), many people mistakenly visualize the face or whole body of the *shaykh*. When someone is doing a Muraqaba of light, he tries to see the color of that light with closed eyes. This is not what imagination (*tassawar*) is. Since that person is trying to see that subject or idea in his mind, the process of viewing is not over yet. As long as you keep beholding, imagination will not form.

The real idea behind imagination is that you should surrender all your thoughts and then just focus on a single thought or idea. You should not put meaning into that thought nor should try to see anything. For instance if you are doing a Muraqaba of your teacher then after closing your eyes, you should concentrate as if you were focusing on your spiritual teacher or your teacher as the center of your attention. You should avoid imagining the facial or physical features of the teacher. Similarly, on Muraqaba of lights, imagine lights are shining on you. Do not focus on the color or the types of lights they are.

In the beginning you are going to have a hard time focusing on that single idea during Muraqaba; you would be inundated with a throng of different thoughts right from the time you start the Muraqaba. The more you try to calm the mind, the greater the influx of thoughts occurs which leads to mental fatigue and boredom. On some occasions the thoughts become so severe that you will have no choice but to end the Muraqaba prematurely. Sometimes it leads to a feeling that one does not have the ability to do Muraqaba, which is of course is nothing but a superstition.

Here the analogy of a horse would best clarify it. Just like a horse, which at first gives stiff resistance to any attempt to tame it, but later gives in, the mind also needs persistent hard work to control it. When you perform Muraqaba in a timely fashion with all the necessary requirements, then the willpower will eventually take hold and the unruly horse of mind will finally submit.

In our consciousness life there are a number of examples in which the attention, despite all the thoughts remains focus on one given idea. In the following examples, we would like to clarify "imagination" during Muraqaba.

EXAMPLE-1: Two people are in love with each other. When mutual love between the two is established then they increasingly spend time thinking about the other. Their thoughts do interchange, however it does not affect the normal routine of daily life.

EXAMPLE-2: A working mother goes to work, leaving her sick child at home. The worrisome thoughts about her child constantly stay on her mind. While at work she performs her duties diligently, however the very thought of her sick child never leaves her mind.

EXAMPLE-3: When columnists begin writing an article or essay, they shift their entire focus towards that essay, the details of the subject matter, sentence structure and so on. Their senses work in many dimensions. Their eyes are fixed on the paper, their hands hold the pen, and their ears keep hearing the surrounding sounds. The sense of touch feels the chair on which the writer is sitting. The sense of smell is able to smell anything and everything around. But despite all this, the attention is never diverted to anything besides the essay, and eventually the essay takes form on that piece of paper.

EXAMPLE-4: Too often, we deal with worrying or distressing thoughts. In this condition we manage to perform more or less all our daily routines but that worrisome thought keeps knocking in our mind. The extent of worry depends on the depth of the thought. Even in this state we do eat, walk, socialize, sleep, and so on. However, if we analyze the mental state, we know that though dormant, that worrisome thought is still active. Sometime the worrisome thought becomes so overwhelming that we isolate ourselves from the environment and become withdrawn.

In the above example we showed that even with all the physical activities and thoughts, the mind is usually focused on something else. In the same manner during Muraqaba the mind keeps focusing on one idea regardless of the other incoming thoughts. During Muraqaba different thoughts descends into the mind without intention. It is the duty of the person doing Muraqaba to keep himself or herself focused on the given idea or imagination without paying attention to the incoming thoughts.

The main reason behind the influx of unrelated thought is the resistance of the consciousness. The human consciousness does not easily accept any practice that it is not used to. When someone surrenders to the conscious resistance; then he or she has gone astray from the path of Divine Guidance (*siraat musta'qeem*). But when he or she keeps on doing Muraqaba without paying attention to the conscious resistance then gradually the flow of incoming thoughts weakens and the feelings of confusion and apathy go away. The easiest way of achieving success in Muraqaba is to avoid fighting or rejecting the thoughts instead simply let them come and go. When you reject a thought repeatedly, it starts echoing itself which leaves a much deeper mark of it in the mind.

EXAMPLE-5: You leave your home for a stroll in the park. You remain aware of the fact that you are heading towards the park. If your brain deletes this idea then you would never be able to reach the park. On your way to the park you come across beautiful houses, street lined with trees, sometimes even garbage in the streets. Nevertheless, regardless of what you see, you are not distracted and keep on going towards the park. If for some reason you had decided to stop to see a beautiful house or to show your disgust at the garbage, you would not have reached the park. On the other hand, if the thought of that beautiful house or that repulsive garbage overwhelms your mind then you would not be able to enjoy the park even after on reaching it.

These examples show that during Muraqaba either rejection of the incoming thoughts or the picture making would plunge your mind in the secondary nonessential thoughts and you would not be able to achieve the needed mental focus.

Avoidance

In the beginning do not practice Muraqaba for too long or too frequently. Moderation is a better course of action. Extremism could lead to apathy, which in turn would lead to avoidance. It is possible for you to become overwhelmed by confusion and apathy and even stop practicing it altogether. Therefore, in the early days keep the duration of the Muraqaba to a minimum (average 15-20 minutes) and gradually increase it, when the need arise. It is also important to perform Muraqaba in a timely fashion. Some people have the tendency to do long Muraqaba some days, while on other days, short ones, and then some days they even miss it.

Consciousness tries its best to end the practice of Muraqaba once and for all. Sometimes we feel fatigue and think about postponing it until the next day. While on other days we think that we did not have a good night's sleep and so we should sleep earlier that day. Sometimes a thought comes to our mind that instead of today we will start the practice the next day and so we keep missing the practice every day.

Often people complain about the environment or the lack of improved conditions. Of course, for every work, a stable condition and environment is needed. However, the consciousness uses that as an excuse to avoid the practice altogether. When the said condition finally improves the person comes up with any other excuse. When we try to fulfill any wish or accomplish something then we usually do that regardless of any resistance or difficulty. When we are drowsy then we get to sleep even in noisy surroundings. When we are late to work then we miss breakfast and head to work. For our regular job, we get up early in the morning; whether we would like it or not we go to work anyway.

If you want the benefits of Muraqaba, you ought to find time for it just as you do for other important matters. When we look at the daily routine of our life, we realize that after daily economic and social business, we waste a noticeable amount of time being idle, worrying, or engaging in unworthy activities. Despite that, we end up whining that there is not much time left for us to do anything extra. When on the one hand you want to get all the benefits of Muraqaba but can not find the time to do it, you are simply deceiving yourself. You truly do not want to do Muraqaba anyway.

Muraqaba and Sleep

Do not combine Muraqaba and sleep. This means that you should avoid doing Muraqaba when you are feeling groggy. If there is mental or physical fatigue then perform Muraqaba after a short rest or nap so the regular program should continue and sleep should not take over. To get rid of nervous and physical fatigue, close your eyes before starting Muraqaba and let the body relax. Slowly take a deep breath and imagine the waves of energy are entering your body. Keep on doing this for a few minutes to remove the physical and mental fatigue.

After completing the Muraqaba, keep on sitting in the same position for a short while. Once Muraqaba is ended the mental focus changes with it. Just as even after waking up the effects of sleep linger on for a while then gradually wakefulness takes over. In the same manner after the Muraqaba leave the mind free so the state of Muraqaba gradually enters the state of wakefulness. After that, walk around the room and avoid conversation. When talking becomes necessary, keep your voice low. Following these instructions will bring the effects of Muraqaba more into wakefulness.

In spirituality, long sleep is frowned upon. It creates stagnation in the mind. That is why we encourage moderation in sleep. Though less sleep helps in the progress of the student of spiritual sciences, for an ordinary person or the beginner duration of sleep should not be too short. Duration of sleep should be based on physical and mental needs. On average six hours of sleep should be enough.

Some people have the habit of reading magazines or books in their bed before sleeping. The downside of this habit is that its mark is absorbed by the mind and is echoed during the sleep. This habit of mind could be used in a favorable way. That is to do Muraqaba before going to bed so that its influence will be prevalent during sleep. We clarified earlier that mixing Muraqaba and sleep should better be avoided. This is to say that during Muraqaba, sleep should not be imposed intentionally. That is why it is important that you should perform Muraqaba in a sitting position and after finishing it, you can go to straight to bed.

Eat easily digestible and simple food. In addition, be careful not to indulge in overeating. A person, who eats food slightly less than his or her full appetite, feels lighter and mental concentration remains high. From a medical point of view as well, greasy, hard to digest food and hot spices are bad for overall health. In short, follow moderation in intake of food as well. Avoid Muraqaba or any other spiritual exercises when you are full. It should be done at least two and half-hours after the last meal.

Storage of Energy

We are always connected with the universal (*cosmic*) mind. Through Muraqaba this cosmic energy is stored in abundance in our mind. Once stored, this energy should be used correctly. That is why it is imperative to avoid all the habits and mental states that waste that stored up energy. This energy is instrumental in Muraqaba and it activates those senses that open in the spiritual realm.

If we are not going to control our mental state then the energy will flow from the higher (*a'ala*) to the lowest (*iss'fal*) senses and eventually be lost in the lower senses. That is why the mind needs to be controlled and focus on one point as much as possible. In the beginning apathy, confusion and irritability come to play and you feel heaviness or burden but later on it gets normal.

Lowering nervous tensions and mental pressures are also important. By using the power of the will, the mind should be concentrated and detached so it will get less involved in the mental confusions. There are information items that bring sadness and there are those that bring happiness. In both conditions control your emotions. Avoid actions that cause the loss of nervous energy; for example speaking loudly, irritability, anger, apathy, unnecessary worries, over zealous sexual tendencies and so on. Apply moderation in all these matters to control the mental aptitude. Having increasing control over the different actions of the mind leads to a condition in which the mind becomes submissive to the will.

The mind remains active subconsciously all the time and it influences all our activities. When the mind accepts the influence of Muraqaba then even subconsciously it remains focused. However, factors like the way of thinking, environment, and worry are hurdles to this focused state. It is impossible to control the effect of environment beyond a certain point. However, you can change the way of thinking so that the mental concentration is not compromised. Patience, thankfulness, faith, reliance, and detachment are those qualities that free the mind from doubts and worries and take it to the highest level. By adopting good manners and courtesy, you can move the mind away from evil and lower thoughts. By using the will power, you can keep the mind away from undesired and evil thoughts. When you are confused, you will remain confused wherever you may go.

Divide the daily routine so the mind will not go astray by being idle for long. Spend free time on positive hobbies and avoid waste of the mental and physical energy on trivial activities. Reading good books of knowledge or of literature, writing, painting, or similar activities are helpful. Engage in routine exercises and athletics. Avoiding banal talk helps in increasing spiritual knowledge.

19
Helpful Exercises

In the field of spiritual sciences there are a number of exercises besides Muraqaba that enhance mental concentration. These exercises help reduce the flow of negative thoughts, which in turn lessens the mental confusion. When these extra exercises are done along with the Muraqaba then mind gains the needed mental focus ahead of time and the positive effects of Muraqaba emerge earlier as well.

Although there are plenty of these exercises available, in this chapter we are going to list only those that are easy to practice and their success rate are also great.

Breathing

In the emotional ups and downs and in the overall nervous system, breathing has a very essential role. During different emotional states, the rate of respiration fluctuates. In tragic circumstances breathing could become a challenge as people often feel difficulty in breathing after hearing tragic news. On the other hand, during anger the rate goes up. During peaceful moments the style of breathing becomes totally different. During this state, breathing becomes balanced and its rate goes down. However when something suddenly comes as a shock then we all simply gasp for air.

Spiritual abilities and breathing are closely interrelated. According to spiritual science, breathing has two sides, ascending and descending. Inhaling is ascending movement while exhaling is descending. During the ascending mode, the person is closer to his or her spiritual state and in the descending mode moves towards the gravity. We are closer to our spiritual state when the inhaling is prolonged and the breath is retained longer then usual.

When respiration stops then our link to the body is disconnected. That is why in order to enter the sub-consciousness senses, breathing does not have to be stopped, but it must be slowed down. A living example is dreaming or a state of deep trance. In these conditions, a person does respire, however the style of breathing is noticeably different from that of a normal breathing pattern. The rate of breathing is slower and the inhaling takes longer as well. Exhaling on the other hand is short-ened. In other words, when we are under the influence of inner senses not only our breathing slows down but the duration of inhaling increas-es as well.

When this style of breathing is intentionally practiced then the sub-conscious state falls on the consciousness during the awakened state and its effects usually last longer.

PRACTICE-1: Sit in a squatting position. Keep your back straight; however, avoid having any part of the body tense. Exhale from both nos-trils so that the lungs are free from air. Slowly inhale through nostrils. When the lungs the lungs become full, exhale through the mouth with-out holding it. During exhaling keep your lips round as if whistling, without holding it. This exhaling and inhaling constitute one cycle. At the beginning start with eleven cycles and gradually go up to twenty-one.

This exercise helps in controlling the movements of lung muscles and it increases the duration of inhaling. The rate of respiration during Muraqaba should be as low as possible. However, it is imperative that the rate of breathing should not be slowed intentionally. Otherwise, the focus would shift to the respiration instead of the Muraqaba. The best way to avoid that is to inhale and exhale slowly for a while before start-ing Muraqaba. That way the respiratory rate will drop automatically.

PRACTICE-2: Sit in a squat position just as in practice-1 and put your forearms on the knees. Inhale slowly from both nostrils. When the lungs are full of air then hold the breath for five seconds. Then exhale through the mouth similar to whistling style. After a few moments rest repeat the process for five times. Next day increase the total to seven until the total number of cycles reaches eleven. At this point, increase the hold period from five to six seconds however the total number of cycles will remain eleven. When holding the breath for six seconds is not causing any men-tal or physical strain then increase it to seven seconds. Unless and until one reaches full command of the practice, keep the hold period to seven seconds. Gradually it should be increased to fifteen seconds, which the maximum allowed time for hold.

PRACTICE-3: After sitting in the squat position as explained in the practice-1, closed the right nostrils using the right hand thumb and inhale through the left nostril for four seconds. Hold it for four seconds. Now using the last two fingers of your hand closed the left nostril while the right nostril is still closed with the thumb. In this way, the remain-ing two middle fingers will be resting between the eyebrows. At this point release only the thumb from the right nostril and exhale from that nostril for four seconds and without stopping inhale from it for four seconds. Again, hold it for four seconds and close the right nostril with the thumb. Then from the left nostrils release those fingers and exhale for four seconds. This constitutes one cycle. After a few moments rest repeat it three times. Increase one cycle every day until you reach seven cycles.

When doing seven cycles and four-second routine becomes comfortable, increase only the hold time to six seconds while the number of cycles will remain at seven. When holding the breath for six seconds and total numbers of cycles is done with ease then increase only the hold time for two more seconds and keep it increasing until the hold time reaches sixteen seconds.

When the seven cycles and holding time of sixteen seconds get easy then increase the exhale time to eight seconds. Final figures should be four seconds inhaling, sixteen seconds holding and then eight seconds exhaling.

Continue practicing with these figures.

All respiratory exercises should be performed at least two and half-hours after a moderate meal. The best time for doing breathing exercises is pre-dawn. At that time not only we are mentally and physically alert but the ratio of oxygen in the air is also the highest. The electro-magnetic activity in the atmosphere is also at its zenith during that time. The second best time for breathing exercises is before going to bed at night.

IS'TAGHRAAQ (immersion):

There are different types of istaghraaq exercises. In one of the styles of the exercises, attention is focused on a physical movement. Since the consciousness is familiar with the physical movements, attaining concentration is easier. By seeing the same movement repeatedly, the consciousness enters the state of immersion *(is-tagh-raaq)*. For example, attention is focused on inhaling and exhaling through different methods.

In other methods of *istaghraaq*, fixing the eyeballs in one position is practiced. The aim is to gain control over the movements of the optical nerves. Once the control is achieved then those movements are frozen at will. This helps in achieving consciousness immersion *(istaghraaq)*.

EXERCISE-1: Lie down on a carpeted floor or on a comfortable bed. The bed should not be too soft. Place your hands beside your body, palms facing upward. Feet should be at least six to twelve inches apart. Let your entire body relax. There should not be any tensions in the nerves. Close your eyes and shift the focus to the right toe. After that move your focus to the left toe.

EXERCISE-2: Sit in a squat position. Keep your back straight and place your palms on your knees. Head should be straight in the direction of the nose. Shift your focus to a point at least two feet away from your feet. Now focus on the inhaling and exhaling and start counting each breath. Each set of inhaling and exhaling will constitute one cycle. During the breathing, the eyes should be fixed on the floor. It is imperative that breathing not be forced. Normal breathing is recommended. Counting should end at ten. When the mind moves its focus away from the breathing, then softly move your focus back to breathing, and restart from first count. If the count to ten is finished without losing focus then do one more round of ten; totaling the count to twenty. After that keep adding ten counts until the total reaches a hundred count. At this point do three rounds of hundreds. The final exercise should be over in five minutes.

EXERCISE-3: This exercise is the advanced form of exercise-2. In this exercise instead of counting the breath, focus is on the breathing itself. It should be noted that even in this exercise breathing should be done in a normal way. Close your eyes and when inhaling, imagine that the air is entering through the nose to chest in the form of a light. During exhaling, imagine that the light is leaving the chest through the nose. Do this exercise slowly and with patience. Again inhale and exhale using the imagination of light.

EXERCISE-4: This exercise will be performed in a dark room. The darker the room the better. Sit in a squat position and fix your eyes at any given point. Do not blink. In the beginning blinking will happen and the eyes get watery as well but after a few days the focus will be achieved. After finishing the exercise close your eyes for few moments and let your mind be free of any thoughts so that the optical nerves get some rest. After that, wash your eyes with cold water.

NOTE: The duration of Exercises 3 and 4 is from five to ten minutes.

EXERCISE-5: Sit in a squat position. Keep your face straight at first and then move a little upward. Shift your focus to the tip of your nose. During this time, the eyes should be half open. At first, the optical nerves will feel tension and the eyes will get watery. The best way to control the tension is to slightly close your eyes. Keep in mind not to create the optical tension intentionally. If the eyes get very teary and are hurting then close your eyes for a while, then reopen, and keep the focus on the tip of the nose. Eventually the optical nerves get used to it and the focus is achieved without any hassle. The duration of this exercise is five minutes as well. Begin with one minute and gradually increase it to five minutes.

20
16-Week Program

Every Muraqaba gives you the needed peace of mind and higher concentration. However, this 16-week program is especially designed to give you even more.

When this sixteen-week program is followed the way it is recommended, it results in removing and curing the following mental disorders and other diseases while achieving desired objectives as well.

FIRST MONTH: (1-4 WEEKS)

Feelings of peace and harmony.
Freedom from stress and worries.

SECOND MONTH: (5-8 WEEKS)

Freedom from fear and anxiety.
End of hypertension.

THIRD MONTH: (9-12 WEEKS)

Heightened immunity and improved health.

FOURTH MONTH: (13-16 WEEKS)

Deep, more relaxed sleep.

FOLLOWING IS THE 16-WEEK PROGRAM

1-4 Weeks:
    Get up early in the predawn hours of the morning and after getting fresh up do the following:

1. Do the breathing exercise (No.1) and then...
2. Lie down on the floor or bed and do the *istaghraaq* practice (No.1).

Your head should be facing north. Do this practice for ten minutes.
3. After that do the Muraqaba and in it imagine lights of blue color are shining on your head. The duration of the Muraqaba is 15 minutes.
4. Before going to bed at night, repeat the *istaghraaq* practice No.1 for ten minutes and after that go straight to bed without talking to anyone.

5-8 Weeks:
The morning after having done the breathing exercise do the *istaghraaq* practice No.2. After that do the *istaghraaq* practice No.1 and imagine lights of green color are falling on you like raindrop.

Before going to bed repeat *istaghraaq* practice No.1, go straight to bed without talking, and do the Muraqaba of the light of pink color.

9-12 Weeks:
Program of 5-8 weeks will continue.

13-16 Weeks:
The same program will continue except that after the breathing exercise instead of the istaghraaq practice, perform the following exercise.

Sit in the squat position and slowly inhale and imagine that through breath waves of energy and health are coming inside your body from the atmosphere and are being absorbed. Exhale without holding the breath. The duration of the exercise is five minutes.

Food Precautions
Avoid Fatty foods, hard-to-digest meals, spicy and high sodium diet. Seasonal fruits and vegetables are strongly recommended.

SELF-IMPROVEMENT

The following program is developed to improve the personality and to create magnetic attraction in an individual. Practice each program for a month.

Program-1: Get up early in the morning before sunrise and practice breathing exercise no.1. After the breathing exercises lie down on floor or a bed. Spread your legs while hands will be beside the body, palms facing upward. Inhale slowly from both nostrils and imagine magnetic waves from the South Pole are going through your body to the north. Imagine that these waves after reaching the North Pole are going back to the south. 5. While you are imagining the magnetic waves going south, exhale. In other words, you have to imagine those waves as a circle. 6. During imagination, the northbound waves will travel through you, however the southbound will travel outside you. 7. On the first day of this exercise, the duration will be five minutes. Increase it gradually to ten minutes.

Program-2: The first month program will continue to the following month.

Program-3: Continue the breathing exercises and the Muraqaba of waves. After these two exercises, do the solar watch exercise (*shughul aftaabi*). Do this exercise after the previous exercise and Muraqaba. The sun has the central and most important position in our solar system and is a source of light and energy. Its light is instrumental in preserving life on our planet. Animal and plants alike benefit from it. Over the years, the spiritual masters have created various methods to store and use as much solar energy as possible. These methods help not only the nervous system but also create magnetism. A strong and energetic nervous system is essential in both worldly and spiritual matters.

The easiest and safest method of *shughul aftaabi* is as follows: Before the sun rises, stand at a higher place, which could be a roof, top, hill, bridge or terrace. Depending on the place, either sit in a squat position or stand straight. You should be facing the sun. The moment the sun rises from the horizon, close your eyes and start to focus on it. Slowly inhale and imagine the energy of the sun entering your body in the form of sunlight. When your lungs become full, imagine the solar energy is all over your body and then slowly exhale. On the first day do this exercise for one minute. After every ten days increase by one minute to a maximum of three minutes. Do this exercise even in cloudy weather. The only difference is that you are going to imagine the Sun on the horizon and your body is absorbing its energy.

Program-4: Stop the breathing exercise no.1 and do no.2 instead. All other exercises will continue.

Food Precautions

Avoid greasy and spicy foods. Boiled meal is recommended, and olive oil can be used in small quantities. Stop smoking. Maximum allowance for tea or coffee is two cups a day.

Immunity

When we look into our daily routine, it becomes obvious that most of the time our nervous system remains under stress. Hurrying to work, traffic jams, pollution, and office politics all contribute to this stress. Different social and domestic matters also occupy our mind. Bright lights at night and the habit of staying up late at night do not let the nerves and muscles relax fully. All this contributes to lower immunity and the organs of the body fail to perform fully. Eventually we become vulnerable to different diseases and ailments.

Should we be able to avoid all these negative factors in our lives and to find time so our nervous and bodily functions can work efficiently, then our improved immunity will be able to fight those diseases.

Mental Weakness

To overcome any nervous weakness, the Muraqaba of the blue light has proven to be highly effective. Following is the recommended program for that:

Get up early in the morning before sunrise and sit in the squat position facing the North. Do breathing exercise no.1 and then close your eyes. Imagine the lights of blue color falling on your head like raindrops. Duration of the Muraqaba is between 15-20 minutes. Repeat this Muraqaba before going to bed at night. Within a few weeks, results will come however, for best results do this for a few more months.

21
Spiritual Concept of Healing

When all diseases and ailments are counted their total exceeds hundreds. The nature and causes of these ailments vary. According to the "spiritual concept of healing" all diseases and ailments consist of two sides. One is physical and the other is either mental or spiritual. Extremities and other physical or chemical changes in the body cause sickness. Based on the spiritual concept of healing, all diseases have forms and figure and spiritual existence. These two sides do coexist. Because of the rise of psychological and physical ailments in our time, it is no longer difficult to grasp this idea. According to this spiritual idea, disease should be attacked not only on its physical side but also on its spiritual or mental side. When it is mentally negated, healing happens quickly. Not only healing is achieved but often complicated and incurable diseases are cured as well.

Since the spiritual side of diseases is not the subject matter of this book, we are only going to present a practical program through which healing power can be stored as much as possible in any individual. The more the storage, the more concentrated will be the power of faith of the patient, resulting in faster healing. Following is the program itself:

Go to bed early at night and get up early in the morning at least half hour before *Fajr* prayer.

After *wudu*, practice breathing exercise-1. Let your mind be free of any thought and do *dhikr* (invocation) of the Divine Name- Ya Hafeez'u (*the Protector*) until the start of the Fajr prayer time.

After Fajr prayer, do Muraqaba imagining you are sitting inside the Divine Throne (*arsh elahii*) and the lights of the Divine Name (*Ya Shaafi-The Healer*) are falling on you. Keep this Muraqaba for at least ten to fifteen minutes.

Within a few months of doing this Muraqaba the patient is able to recover from the ailment and eventually becomes healthy.

22

Muraqaba of Colored Lights

E verything that exists in this world is dominated by one or more colors. Nothing is of no color. Chemistry reveals that if any element goes through changes, it emits specific colors. This order of the colors is the basic characteristic of any element. That is why in every element the order of colors is different. The same rule applies to humans as well. A well-organized system of colors and waves works in humans. The balance of those colors and waves controls the overall health of the individual. Changing of color affects the mood of the individual as well.

Colors also play an important role in the fields of emotions and feelings. It is our daily observation that when someone hears bad or tragic news, he or she gets pale. Fear also changes the color while during anger, eyes and face becomes red.

When the color of the room is red, it creates a feeling of burden or heaviness but if the same room is colored blue then peace and serenity is felt. Greenery and colorful flowers help us get rid of mental and physical fatigue. However, when the same trees become leafless during autumn our feelings change as well.

The theory of colors and lights states that those specific amounts of colors are prevalent not only in the physical body of humans but also in their senses. If for any given reason, the system of colors is changed or any specific color is increased or decreased or their ratio is changed, it leads to a change of feelings and emotions in an individual.

In the spiritual sciences, the color code is intentionally changed in a student so that his or her mind could come close to the subconscious senses. Continued practice of Muraqaba also helps in improving coloration in the senses. It is imperative that changes in the colors be done solely to improve or to awaken any specific skill. When supplementing colors and lights are not used to improve any specific sense, then normal senses are affected by it. A spiritual master always keeps his eyes on the progress of his student. When needed he can adjust the ratio of colors using his spiritual discretion (*tasarraf*) so that the consciousness remains functional with those changes in colors and light.

On the other hand, when these changes occur in an individual abnormally then the body malfunctions and usually manifests in physical or psychological disorders. These disorders are usually labeled as general diseases or ailments like hypertension, anemia, asthma, cancer, arthritis, nervous and sensory or emotional disorders.

According to the spiritual sciences, only an expert spiritual master decides what color of light needs changing. In these decisions the personality type, mental strength, way of thinking, physical form and other factors are taken into consideration.

Using Muraqaba, the following are the different methods of absorbing light of any particular color in an individual.

METHOD-1: Sit in a comfortable position and imagine the waves of color and light and being absorbed by the whole body.

METHOD-2: During the Muraqaba imagine that from the sky the waves of color and light are falling and are being absorbed into your brain.

METHOD-3: During the Muraqaba imagine the entire surrounding environment lit with the same light.

METHOD-4: Imagine that you are immersed in the river of that light.

Medically and physiologically, each color of light has its own attributes. When the Muraqaba of a certain color of light is performed, it causes chemical changes in the brain, which enables it to absorb as much as possible the light of that color. Since medical and psychological disorders are not the subject matter of this book we are not going to discuss this matter in detail. However, we will present Muraqabas of color and light for such psychological disorders that occur because of mental confusions and paranoia.

NOTE: The decision, of what color of light Muraqaba is to be given must be made by no other than a spiritual master.

BLUE LIGHT:

Blue lights are instrumental in getting rid of mental disorders, neck and back pain, vertebra malfunctions, depression, inferiority complex, and weak willpower. The correct way to do the Muraqaba is as follows:

Imagine that you are sitting beneath the sky and the blue light is falling from the sky into your head and after passing through your entire body is going to the earth through the feet.

Case History

Mr. Jamiluddin from Lahore, Pakistan wrote:

I have been doing the Muraqaba of blue lights for my back and neck pain as prescribed by you. The first day the image of blue lights was a bit dim but the next day I felt a stream of blue light entering my brain from the sky. I felt my whole brain was filled with that light. Then these lights entered my heart, then through the stomach went to my feet, and finally were descending through the floor. My vision went towards the light, which was entering the ground. I felt as if the lights leaving my body were more impure than the one entering my body. A thought came to my mind that the exiting lights are taking the ailment with them. After doing this Muraqaba for about 15 minutes I felt light. After the end of the Muraqaba I also felt the pain had lessened. Now after a whole month of doing the Muraqaba, the pain is gone.

Ms. Razia Sultana from Tando Adam, Sindh wrote:

For the last three years, I had depression. I used to get hopelessness all the time without any obvious reason. I was aware of happiness but my life was void of it.

The Muraqaba of blue light has turned my world upside down. Within six weeks of continuing Muraqaba I am feeling happy after a long time. Obviously, the blue lights have turned away the waves of sadness from me.

Muhammad Hamid from Karachi, Pakistan wrote:

I am twenty years old and a college student. My willpower is so weak that I have become impractical. I do not have the confidence of initiating conversation with anyone in college. I have not been able to correct this problem...please help!

The author of this book prescribed the Muraqaba of blue light for him. A month later he responded in these words:

Dear Shaykh Azeemi,

No doubt, you do care for the creatures of God. Your prescribed blue color Muraqaba has revolutionized my life. During this past one month, my personality is totally changed. Now I am a normal healthy young man. I have great confidence. Below is the short version of my Muraqaba report.

REPORT:

On the first day, I was not able to concentrate. A stream of thoughts kept coming to my mind. Acting on your advice I did not pay attention to them. Then one day the image of the sky appeared and the blue light. Then for the next few days, the image appeared as if the blue lights from the sky were shining on my head like a searchlight and being absorbed by my heart. Then after that for a few days I saw my whole body is made of blue lights. I noticed that after each Muraqaba I felt very light. Slowly and steady, I was able to gain confidence and now I can talk to anyone like a normal person. I am feeling though a new me is born. I am still practicing the blue-light Muraqaba and planning to keep on doing it for a while.

YELLOW LIGHT:

Muraqaba of the yellow light is effective is curing digestive disorders such as gas, intestinal pain, dysentery, constipation, pyria, stomach ulcers, and similar symptoms.

Case History

Salma Choudhry from Multan wrote,

"I had stomach ulcer for over two years. You told me to do Muraqaba of yellow-light, which I did. I was imagining that I was sitting beneath the sky and the lights of yellow color were falling into my head and were finally being stored in the stomach and the ulcer was being removed by it. For two weeks, I sensed that those lights are gradually reducing the ulcer. On the third week while doing Muraqaba, a thought crossed my mind that the ulcer had been removed and now only the bright yellow lights were in my stomach. It has been a month since but I still get those feelings during muraqba. I am no longer taking medicine for the ulcer and doing only the yellow-light Muraqaba. I do not know how to thank you. You have given me a new life."

Mansoor Ahmed from Kakra Town wrote,

"I had chronic dysentery for a long period of time. I went to different doctors but it was not cured. I had almost lost all hope of being cured when a friend of mine suggested that I should contact you. After listening to my ordeal, Shaykh Azeemi suggested that I should do the Muraqaba of yellow lights, and God willing, I will be cured. I was a little skeptical when I first started because I had seen many well-known

doctors and spent a fortune on it as well. For years, I was on a strict diet. I could not believe that this simple treatment would solve the problem. Nevertheless, I started the Muraqaba, but for the first two days I was not able to concentrate at all. On the third day however, the image of yellow light was eventually formed and I gained interest in the Muraqaba. After a couple of weeks, the image was fully formed and I started feeling the lights inside me. During this period the dysentery also stopped and I abstained from bad food as well. My appetite has increased as well."

Another gentleman from Lahore wrote,

"For the last three years I was inflicted with intestinal pain. I went to a different doctor but the only way I could avoid the pain was to be on strict diet. Finally, I was told to do Muraqaba of yellow light. The burning sensation and the pain are almost gone. The other day I went to a doctor who said I no longer have the disease. I could not tell you how happy I was on that day. Now in every social gathering I tried to discuss the Muraqaba with the friends and family. In my view the best form of thankfulness is to promote the use of Muraqaba so that more and more people could benefit form it."

ORANGE LIGHT:

It is best recommended for chest ailments such as chronic cough, asthma, ulceration of the lungs, and tuberculosis.

Case History

A female patient had chronic ulceration of the lungs. The disease had reached a point where she was vomiting blood. She was told to do Muraqaba of orange lights with massage of orange-light oil. Within two months the frequency of the blood vomiting dropped. After six months of the treatment, she was completely cured.

Mr. Athar Husayn from Phalia, Pakistan wrote,

"I have had asthma for the past twelve years and now am hopeless. I am writing you with hope that you will pay attention to my misery."

He was also told to do Muraqaba of orange-light and was given the water made with orange-light. By the grace of God the twelve-year-old disease finally ended.

GREEN LIGHT:

Muraqaba of green light is given to treat hypertension, skin disorders such as itching, eczema, discoloration of skin, gonorrhea, and syphilis.

Case History

Nasrullah Baig from Mardan wrote,

"I had itching all over my body. For three years, I got treatment at various places. However, often the itching turned into a wound and the pain was agonizing. Nevertheless after doing Muraqaba of green-light for six months I was fully cured by it."

Naheed Fatima from Mianwali, Pakistan wrote,

"I had severe high blood pressure for a while. Sometimes it gets so bad that even performing daily routines would become a challenge. My small children were affected by the condition as well. By doing Muraqaba of green-light every morning and before going to bed and having a green light bulb in my bedroom at night, my blood pressure came to normal within twenty days."

Sundus Batool from Peshawar, Pakistan wrote,

"Discoloration of the skin was my problem. It made me self-conscious and I had extreme inferiority complex. Green-light Muraqaba has cured my condition."

RED LIGHT:

The Muraqaba of red-light is given to treat low blood pressure, depression, anemia, arthritis, low energy, cowardice, nervous breakdown, hopelessness, fear of death etc.

Case History

Dr. Niaz Hussein wrote,

"For the past twelve months my wife was the victim of nervous breakdowns. In medicine, tranquilizers usually are given to treat this disorder. Sleep helps in removing the nervous tension, however; the

downside is that it is habit-forming. I gave my wife those sleeping pills for six months but then she became addicted to them. Stopping the medicine would always result in even more severe seizures. Finally, I told her to do the Muraqaba of red light. No doubt, Muraqaba is the most effective and harmless way of treatment. Now I often prescribe Muraqaba my own patients besides giving them medicines so humanity would get benefit from it."

Mr. Sibghatullah wrote,

"My mind always had thoughts of hopelessness. There were no obvious reasons for it. For some reason, I was always thinking negatively. With red-light Muraqaba my thinking has now changed to positive."

VIOLET LIGHT:

It is given to treat male sexual dysfunction such as impotence, loss of libido and female uterine disorders.

Case History

A gentleman from DIG Khan, Pakistan wrote,

"Because of erectile dysfunction I was not fit to marry anyone. Consequently, I had an inferiority complex. Muraqaba of purple lights and the massage of purple-light oil have pretty much removed this weakness from me."

A woman from Chichawatani, Pakistan wrote,

"I have been married for five years but was childless. Doctors had told me that my uterus was swollen. I went through different treatments but with no results. Finally the Muraqaba of violet light and the massage with its oil has removed the uterine swelling and I am now pregnant."

PINK LIGHT:

Hysteria, mental seizures, weak memory, paranoia, insecurity, negative thoughts about life, isolation, are treated with Muraqaba of pink light.

Case History

Mr.Salman Ansari from Thatta, Pakistan wrote,

"I used to get seizures all the time. I went through some tough times. Often it happened while I was at the market. Because of falls, I was injured several times as well. On one occasion, it happened during a shower. After about an hour people took notice of that. Thereafter someone was with me all the time. God bless Azeemi Sahib who prescribed for me the Muraqaba of pink light. I have total confidence now that God willing I will be cured by it."

Ms. Seema Nazli from Hyderabad wrote,

"Constant fear and paranoia had filled me with cowardice and an inferiority complex. Life after marriage was such a challenge for me, I was so mortified by my husband and in-laws that even when everything was right I was afraid of something. With this, I also had the fear of God. Every act felt like a sin and I was always repenting with fear of His wrath. All this pressure made me weak and I always felt fatigued. My husband told me to do a Muraqaba of pink light. After doing it for two months, now I am confident that I will be cured."

23
Station of Ihsaan

Recite 100 times the *Darood-Sharif* and 100 times the Divine Name-Ya'Haiyu Ya'Qayyumu and then close your eyes and imagine you are watching God or that God is watching you. This Muraqaba helps create the link between you and God and keeps fear and grief away from you.

The Muraqba of *Ihsaan* is great for forming *Salat* (prayer; remembrance of God). The prophet Muhammad has said," when you standing for prayer, imagine that you are seeing God or that God is seeing you." This Muraqaba creates the link with the Divine and the joy during prayer.

Saadia Khanum from Shah Kot, Pakistan wrote,

"With your permission I started the Muraqaba of Ihsaan. Here is the report:

During Muraqaba, I saw myself beneath the Divine Throne. The floor resembled mercury and there was a comfortable bed for me nearby. I was sitting in it comfortably. Divine Light was falling on me. A thought came that this is the light of Divine Vision and God is watching me. I saw in His vision great love and compassion. I felt like a little girl and I had a desire to see Him. I asked Him, 'When can I see You, O' Lord!'"

He replied, 'Thou art too young to see Us. When thou art old enough then We will grant thee Our glimpse.'

I kept asking questions of when I would be old enough, when this would happen. Then a thought crossed my mind that though I could not see Him, He is watching me, and he understands me. Moreover, when I am older I will be able to see Him. That thought had a calming effect on me. Every cell of my body was feeling serenity and joy."

Rasheed Khan from DG Khan, Pakistan wrote,

"*I started the Muraqaba with the permission of the Sufi Master (author). I saw myself standing under the Divine Throne (ursh) and the Divine Light (nur) is falling on me like a fountain. Its rays entered my head and then were absorbed into my eyes. I felt as if I had a binocular and I could see everything clearly. I saw the Divine Light was encompassing me like a sheet. Every layer felt like a separate sheet as if one were wearing a sheet over another sheet. This clothing of light felt glued to my body. They looked great. There were in total thirty-five sheets all over me and for a long time the Divine Light kept shining into my eyes. Then my vision started seeing the Divine Throne (arsh), suddenly the flow of the light stopped. I felt that God was on the Throne (arsh). I glanced at Him and was lost. Then I felt the Divine Light coming directly out of Him and entering me. This light was even brighter and more delicate than the previous one. With this light my face lit up like a star. I felt Him very close to me. In my mind, I had the echo of the following verse of the Qur'an (Koran):*"

"*We are closer to thee than thy cerebral vein.*"

"*During the entire period of Muraqaba the thought of His nearness and His Light dominated my mind. I felt as though I were made of delicate lights. My heart and mind felt likewise. I felt immensely the Divine Love. I wished I could always be near Him. At that moment besides longing for Him, I had no other thoughts in my mind.*"

NOTE: Seekers of the Truth are required to do this Muraqaba only after obtaining permission from their Spiritual Master (*murshid*).

We mentioned earlier that spirituality creates a condition through which the student is able to feel the Divine Presence to a point where they feel like they are watching God. The program of *salat* (prayer) is meant to reinforce the link with God and the idea that God is omnipresent wherever they may go. When they complete this exercise, the audience with the Divine becomes an observation. The prophet Muhammad has called this state the station of *Ihsaan*.

At least twenty minutes before *Fajr* prayers, sit in a comfortable position. Close your eyes and imagine you are at the Divine Court and God is in front of you. Keep this imagination for five to ten minutes and then form the Fajr prayer. During the prayer keep the imagination that God is in front of you. During prayer, imagine that you are praying in the Divine Court right in front of Him. This way the mind will be focused on God while the body will be performing the prayer. While reciting the Qur'an *(Koran)* during prayer, imagine that you are conversing with God. After completing the prayer, while still sitting keep the imagination of Divine Presence for a few minutes.

If you are having difficulty in imagining God then imagine that you are present before Him and God is witnessing your every movement. Either of the two imaginations can be done. If in the beginning the imagination is not formed then do not worry. Keep practicing this consistently and God willing you soon will be able to establish the image and will feel the real closeness of God during prayers.

Before *Zohr* and *Asr* prayers, do *dhikr* (invocation) of *Al-Lah Haziri* (God is present) *Al-Lah Naziri* (God is seen) for a few minutes and imagine the presence of God. Then continue this imagination during the entire prayer. During *Maghrib*, prayers due to lack of time only do the imagination that you are present before Him.

In the *I'sha* prayer, imagine the presence of God five minutes before the prayer and then perform the prayer. At night before going to bed repeat the imagination of either seeing God or that He is seeing you for ten minutes and then go to sleep.

When you are not enthusiastic about the prayer or you miss it often then for forty days perform the Fajr prayer in the mosque with the congregation. God willing, no more prayers will be missed afterwards.

24

The Hidden World

*S*alat is the name of the prayer in which God's Glory, Majesty, Providence and Rule are acknowledged. It has always been mandatory to all prophets and their followers (*ummah*). By establishing *salat*, the person becomes closer to God. It prevents vulgarity and excesses. *Sala*t, through mental concentration, takes you towards God. Mental concentration is gained through it.

When Abraham sent his son to live near Mecca, he reasoned his decision with God in these words. "O' our Lord! So that they will establish *Salat* (communication with You).

He also prayed for his descendants,

> "O Lord! Make my progeny and me the maker of *Salat*
> (link). "Ishmael always ordered his family to establish
> *Salat*."
> [*Qur'an* (Koran), Chapter- Maryam: 55]

The *Qur'an* (Koran) has mentioned Lot, Isaac, Jacob, and their progeny in these words,

> "We revealed to them to do good deeds and to establish
> the *Salat*." [Chapter-Prophets: 73]

Luqman Advised his son in the following way:

> "O my son, establish *Salat*."
> [*Qur'an* (Koran), Chapter-Luqman: 17]

God said to Moses,

> "For My remembrance, establish *Salat*, connect with
> Me with mental focus."
> [*Qur'an* (Koran), Chapter-Taha: 14]

God ordered Moses, Aaron, and the Israelites to establish the *Salat*.

> "And Al-Lah ordered the *Salat*."
> [*Qur'an* (Koran), Chapter Mary: 31]

It is mentioned in the last scripture *Qur'an* (Koran) that Jews and Christians of Arabia were familiar with *Salat*.

> "Among the People of the Book, there are those who at night recite God's Word while standing and prostrating." [*Qur'an* (Koran), Chapter Family of Imran: 113]

> "And those people who obey the scriptures (Divine Laws) and establish the *salat*, We do not dispose the reward of those who do good deeds."
> [*Qur'an* (Koran), Chapter Aeraaf: 120]

When you connect with God then a door is opened in your mind that takes you to the hidden unseen world to explore it.

By pondering the deeper meaning of *Sala*t and the different aspects of prayer, we are able to realize that *Salat* restores mental concentration.

With improved concentration, you will be able to move out of the conscious state and moves into the subconscious one. That is what the purpose of Muraqaba is all about, to let you get familiar with the subconscious realm, the so called unseen world, with the help of higher concentration. When you are able to connect with God through the *Salat* or prayer then, the whole prayer becomes Muraqaba.

To improve concentration during the prayer and to create a link with God, the following Muraqaba is usually taught.

After performing *wudu*, sit in a comfortable position facing the Ka'aba, recite three times *Darood Sharif*, three times *Kalima Shahada* and then close your eyes. For one minute to three imagine that God is present at the Divine Throne (*arsh*) and the Divine Lights (*tadjalli*) are shining on and you are beneath the Throne. After that, form your prayer.

When you are able to perform the prayer (*Salat*) the way you do Muraqaba then is called Muraqaba of forming *Salat* (*Qayam ul Salat*).

The *Qur'an* (Koran) is the Word of God and is the account of the realities and mysteries that God revealed on the sacred heart of Prophet Muhammad through Archangel Gabriel. Every word of the *Qur'an* (Koran) is the repository of lights and illuminations. Outwardly, the words are in Arabic language, inwardly however, there exists a vast world of illuminating symbols and meanings. In spirituality and *tasawwaf* (Sufism) students receive training to witness through the eyes of the soul the illuminating symbols of the words, so that the *Qur'an* (Koran) could be understood in its entirety and depth. The *Qur'an* (Koran) also states this truth and it encourages the person to grasp it.

Whenever you recite the *Qur'an* (Koran) whether in prayers or during the regular recitation, imagine that through the words of the *Qur'an* (Koran), God is conversing with you and you are listening to the recitation through the angels of the Divine Throne. Imagine that Divine Mercy (*rahma*) is revealing the illuminating symbols of the words to you.

When you recite the *Qur'an* (Koran) with full mental concentration, you link with the source that revealed the *Qur'an* (Koran). Because of it, your heart becomes enlightened with the higher angels of the Divine Throne. This enables your heart to get spiritually clean. The cleaner your heart gets, the more the illuminating world of true meaning of the Word is revealed to you.

25
Muraqaba of Life After Death

Human life does not end with death. After death, the human ego, takes on the form of an illuminating body upon leaving the physical body. Through the illuminating body, it remains active. Much like in dreams, where the physical senses (physical world) become subordinated to the subconscious senses (senses of world of lights) but do not become idle. Our condition during sleep resembles death. However when the dominant senses of body of light take over the senses of physical body in a way that the physical senses are unable to regain dominance then the physical body becomes permanently idle. This is what death is.

The Muraqaba of after life is practiced to recess the physical senses by imposing the senses of the body of light temporarily. When the student becomes skilled then they can suspend their physical senses (consciousness) and let the senses of light (subconscious) take over whenever they wish and vise versa.

There is a famous saying of the Prophet Muhammad:

> "Die, before death clutches thee." This *hadith* also points to this idea of experiencing the life after death while you are still alive and well by simply subordinating your physical senses to the subconscious. This way you can discover the world where souls live after the death of their bodies."

Aeraaf:

Lie down in a comfortable place. Then shift focus to every part of your body to make them relax. Imagine that you are flying in the space in your body of light, heading towards life after death. Gradually the body of light, also known as Aura, becomes activated and is able to witness the realm where humans move after death and to watch their lifestyle.

Let' go and find the secrets of life after death! Sit in a squat position, close your mouth, and inhale slowly through your nostrils and hold. Keep on holding as long as you can then open your mouth and slowly exhale. Imagine the depth of the grave and spiritually step inside the grave.

Below is the author's own account of the observation during the Muraqaba of life after death.

Now we are under the grave...a mixed smell of soil and camphor is all over the place...here the oxygen is so low that it's suffocating...eyes are getting heavy and sleepy...eyelids are still...blinking has stopped...the vision is now focused at one point...right before the eyes we are seeing small and big spring-like circles come towards us...Glory to God! How delightful and colorful the scenery is...how come suddenly it's dark now...I can not even see my hands...

Watch...!

In front of us about two hundred miles away there is a light in the space...there is a door nearby...let's go inside...

Wow! There is a whole city in there...high rise buildings, well-built buildings and others not so great as well. There are bayous and a wash area too. Lush greenery and flowers and trees with fruits as well...in the town there are palaces and stoneage like caves where people live, all in the same place...

I was curious to see what was inside those caves. When I looked inside, it was a very dark cave where human souls were resting. How shameful it was that in this part of the supernatural world everyone was nude. They were not even aware of the idea of clothing. These nude people were watching me in utter amazement. Finally, one of them asked me the reason I bothered to put this load (of clothing) on my soft body, though by appearance I looked just like them.

After a long session of debates, we learned that these souls belong to the time when the inhabitants of the world had no social order and had no idea about the need to cover their private parts.

Magnificent City

This whole city whose population exceeds billions and trillions has been there for millions of years. You can walk around and see the culture and civilization of millions of years. Here there are some people who are not aware of the use of fire and those who are classified in our world as stoneage people. In this city there are some nations who are even more advanced than we are in our scientific and information age. They had created far more advanced aircraft and missiles. Also, in this city there was this intellectual nation which had formulas that negate gravity and were able to reduce the mass of thousands of tons to fewer than that of a pillow for construction purposes.

Also in that city there are those who had control over time and space and were able to know what angels were doing while they were still living on earth. Through their inventions they were able to avert the winds and were able to reduce the intensity of the high winds. In this city, there are the guest of gods in the Heaven and those who are waiting for their turn to become the fuel of Hell.

Here there are fields of crops and marketplace too. In the marketplace, there are shops but no shoppers. Let us go and see what is going on there.

Business

There was this person sitting in his shop, where there were boxes everywhere but nothing was in them. He looked sad and gloomy. I said, "How are you?" He replied, "I am sad because it's been five hundred years and not a single customer has come in yet." After inquiring it was revealed that this person was a capitalist when he was in the earth, profiteering and fraud were his routine.

In the next shop, there was another person, an old one. His hair was dry and uncombed. His face showed signs of fear and anxiety. In front of him were papers and account books. The shop was big and clean. This person was busy calculating something in the book and would say the numbers aloud. He would keep saying the numbers and calculating over and over and every time the final figure would turn out to be wrong. Every time he realized the total was wrong he would start screaming, crying, cursing himself, and then go back to calculating. I asked him, "what are doing and how long have you been doing this?"

He looked at me for a few seconds and said, "I could not tell you my condition. I have been trying to calculate correctly for the past three thousand years but have not been able to do so because in my life I was the accountant and used to cook other people's books."

Evil Religious Leaders

There was this person, the mullah (priest). His beard was long like ropes. When he walks he gathers his beard and wraps it around his hips. But when he starts walking the wrapped beard opens and he falls on his face. To my inquiry he said, "In my life on earth I had a long beard so that I could deceive people. Having a long beard was something I considered important. Through it, I could easily deceive naïve and good people.

Then I saw another person shouting loudly saying, "O people, let me tell you what God has said, come on people I will tell you everything that God has said." No one paid attention to him but I saw a group of angels heading towards him.

They said to him, "Tell us what God has said." The mullah (priest) replied immediately, "I have been thirsty for a long time, give me some water and then I will tell you everything." Then the angels give him hot boiling water. When he refuses, they pour the water on his face and then laugh at him, saying loudly, "Curses on him, he was saying that he is going to tell the word of God. In the world as well he used God's name for his hidden motives. Here he is doing the same." From his burned mouth come unbearable screams. I then went away from him. It was horrible to watch.

Gossip

In this huge city, there is a dark and congested street. At the end of the street, there are fields of crops and jungle. Here there is a house made up of walls and a fishnet like roof. There is no protection from rain or sunlight. In this house, I saw only women. The environment was tense and suffocating. One woman was sitting there. Surprisingly her upper body was normal but her legs were ten feet long.

Seeing her in this misery, I asked her, "Madam, what is going on here?" She said that during her life on earth she was known for gossiping. Now she was incapable of walking and her legs were burning like charcoal. No one was there to sympathize with her.

Backbiting

There was this person walking with fear and had a knife with him. O God, he stabbed another person with his knife and started drinking the blood. Because of drinking the blood he started vomiting. He got very weak and said, "I wish I had known in the finite world that this would be the punishment for backbiting."

Tall Buildings

There were these tall men, about twenty feet tall with wide bodies. Because of their length and width they could not enter any buildings of the area. They were walking, jumping from one roof to the other but were not able to sit and relax. Sometimes they cry or hit their head in distress.

I asked them, "What is going on here, why are you so sad and worried?"

One of them replied, "In the world I seized the rights of orphans and made buildings out of that wealth. These are the same buildings, now their doors are closed to me. Delicious and greasy food has put air and fire in my stomach. The air has made my body so big that I can no longer enter my building and the fire...this fire is burning me. I want to flee but there is no escape."

Now let us see the other side of the life after death.

Angel of Death

During the Muraqaba of life after death, I saw a home at the end of a field. Inside the walls, there is a big tree. There are many people standing under that tree. I went there as well. I saw a woman arguing with someone saying that she would not allow him to take away her husband. That man replied that he could not help her as he was acting on Divine Command. He said, "These are the matters of God, He does what He wishes." The woman then shouted, "Ah!" and began crying. I went ahead and asked the man why he was harassing her. He looked at me and said, "Look at me closely and recognize who I am."

I then closed my eyes the way we do in Muraqaba and tried to see him. I then realized he was the angel of death. I greeted him respectfully and extended my hand for a handshake. The archangel Izraeel shook my hand and I felt as if electricity were going through me. I felt the shocks as well and was knocked down by the force of the current.

I was scared; nevertheless I asked him politely, "What is the matter with her husband?" The archangel Izrael replied, "He is the beloved servant of God. This woman is his wife and she is also a good person. God has commanded this man to leave the world. I was told that I can only collect his soul if he so wishes. He is with the Divine Wish and ready to leave this world, but his wife is insisting that she will not let me take his soul unless they both die together."

Then the angel of death took my hand and we went to a nearby room made of clay. There I saw a holy man lying in a gray colored blanket. The pillow was of leather and inside there were date tree leaves. His beard was short and round. He had a tall muscular body, broad forehead with big bright eyes. One thing I noticed as well was that his forehead was so bright as if the rays of the sun were coming from it. It was so bright that I could hardly stare at it. Upon entering the room the angel of death said to him, "Assalaam Alaykum O' Abdullah (Slave of God)!"

I too said, "Salaam Alaik, Mr. Abdullah!"

Hazarat Abdullah (most likely his name was abdullah as well) then said to the angel of death,

"What order of our Creator have you brought with you?"

The angel replied, "God wishes to see you."

Then the angel sat in front of him in a meditative pose and the holy man slowly lay in front of him. His body shook for a second and then his soul left his body. The angel then departed for the sky. I could see him going up and up...

Muraqaba Nur

According to the spiritual science, the main ingredient of creating this universe is *nur*. There is a verse in the *Qur'an* (Koran):

"God is the *nur* of the skies and the earth."

Nur is that special form of light that not only can be seen but is also a source of guidance to other lights. Light, waves, color, these are all the attributes of *nur*. One of the other main qualities of *nur* is that it can run simultaneously in both the present and the past and connects past and present. If this connection did not going work, then the universe's connection with the past would be disconnected resulting in its annihilation. We can use the analogy of memory here. We are individually and collectively in every moment of our time are connected with our past. When we reminisce about our childhood or any other event of our past then through *nur*, the past enters the present and we are able to remember the events the way they happened. Besides humans, the senses of angels, genies and other creatures are also based on the *nur*. In spirituality the Muraqaba of *Nur* is given to students so that they may familiarize themselves with it. There are several ways of doing this Muraqaba:

The student imagines the entire Universe and its creatures are immersed in the ocean of Nur. The students also imagine themselves being immersed in it.

The students imagine that a stream of *nur* is shining on the entire world from the Divine Throne. The muraqib (student) feel the *nur* is also shining on them.

There is a verse in the *Qur'an* (Koran):

"God is the *nur* of skies and the earth, its example is like a tray in which a lamp is placed and that lamp is inside the case of glass."

[Chapter: Nur]

By using the above example of the *Qur'an* (Koran), the student imagines that their entire body is lit with the light of that lamp.

All the religions of the world speak of an invisible form of light, a light that is the source of all other lights. It is stated in the Bible,

"And when God said light, there was light."

Moses first saw the light in the burning bush in the Sinai and through that light conversed with God. In Hinduism that light is called Jot.

In all the forms of spirituality, the Muraqaba of *nur* is given to practice. Its style is similar to what was described earlier.

26
Kashaf ul Qaboor

After death, life shifts from the material world to the spiritual realm where it continues in a new dimension and the ego remains active in the other world as well. This world is called in the *Qur'an* (Koran) the a*eraaf*. Its condition depends on the deeds of the individual in the material world. If at the time of death one is peaceful and free of mental impurities and filth then his or her state in the hereafter will be peaceful and serene as well. On the other hand, when one leaves this world with anxiety, guilty conscience, or mental suffocation then the same conditions will greet that person in the *aeraaf*.

The Muraqaba of *kashaf ul qaboor* is done on the graveside of the deceased with whom you would like to meet. With this Muraqaba you will be able to not only meet the deceased but also to witness his or her condition in the hereafter.

When this Muraqaba is done at the tomb of saints (*wali*) the purpose is to gain spiritual blessing (*faidh*) from them and a glimpse of them (*ziarat*) as well.

The correct method of performing this Muraqaba is as follows:

Sit towards the end of the grave (as opposed to towards the tombstone). Inhale through the nose slowly and when you are full then exhale slowly without holding the breath. Repeat this eleven times. After that close your eyes and shift your focus inside the grave. After few moments let your mind go deep in the grave, as if that grave were a depth and your attention were falling in it. Keep this focus during the Muraqaba. The esoteric vision will eventually be activated and the soul of the deceased will show up. Depending on the mental capacity and strength, success comes with consistent practice and efforts.

The practice of this Muraqaba should be limited only to the tombs of saints or Imams (*Ahlul Bayt*) for their spiritual sightings (*ziarat*) and the blessings (*faidh*). Unnecessary Muraqaba on the graves of ordinary persons should be avoided.

THE FOLLOWING IS THE AUTHOR'S OWN ACCOUNT OF THE MURAQABA OF KASHAF UL QABOOR:

When I was doing the Muraqaba towards the end of the grave, I saw a layer of soul leave my body and go inside the grave. I saw His Highness Saint Lal Shahbaz Qalander sitting there. The grave looked like a big room. On the left hand side of the grave there was a window or small door. Lal Shahbaz Qalander said to me, "Go see what's inside that door, you are free."

When I opened the door I saw a huge garden. It was so beautiful and glorious that you could not find it anywhere in the world. It had everything. I saw birds whose wings were emitting light, flowers that were so beautiful that they are beyond the scope of human consciousness. There was another unique feature about those flowers that each one was a combination of multiple colors, colors that seemed like tiny lightbulbs. When the wind blows, these colorful flowers create a magnificent scene similar to fireworks. The trees were unique in a way that their stems, branches, flowers, and fruits were all round much like mushrooms. When air flows between them it creates such a melody that one gets lost in it. This garden also had grapes of dark pink and blue colors. Each grape is as big as an apple in our world. The garden also had fountains and milky bayous.

The garden had many birds but I did not see any animals. I asked a parrot who was sitting in a beautiful tree where this park was situated. The parrot replied in a human language that this is heaven and the garden of God's friend Lal Shahbaz Qalander. After saying that, it flew through the air singing hymns. In short, what I saw there is hard to describe in words. I took a branch of grapes and went back to Lal Shahbaz Qalander. The grand Saint asked me if liked the garden. I replied, "Your Highness, no one has ever seen or heard of this garden. I could not even fully appreciate it."

SHAH ABDUL AZIZ DEHALVI:

A great South Asian saint of the nineteenth century Syed Ghauth Ali Shah Qalandar (1804-1880) of Pani Put, India, has recorded the following event in his book *Tazkira-e-Ghauthia* that provides an outstanding and marvelous piece of information about life after death and Aeraaf. This event took place when Syed Ghauth Ali Shah was the disciple of one of the great Sufi Masters of his time Hadrat Syed Shah Abdul Aziz Dehalvi.

Ghauth Ali Shah writes:

A man came to the court of Shah Sahib. By appearance he looked like a royal official. He said to him, "My story is so strange that no one believes me. My own cognition does not work. I do not know what to say, where to go, what to do. Finally I have come in your service."

He then said, "I used to live in Lukhnow. I had a job; things were great. Then my luck went sour and my economic conditions worsened to a point where I became jobless and could not find any work. Then I said to myself that instead of sitting idle why not try my luck in a different city. I took some money for traveling expenses and set off towards Odhaypour. On my way, I rested at a place called Rewari. At the time that place had nothing but a tent and an inn. A few prostitutes used to live there. I was sitting outside the inn wondering what to do because all my money had gone and I was not able to find any work. One of the prostitutes came towards me and asked me why I was not eating, as it was past the dinner hour. I told her I was tired from the journey and would eat after resting. She then went back to the inn. A few hours later she came back and asked the same question and I gave her the same reply. Nevertheless, on the third time when she asked me I told her the whole story how I had ran out of the money and now I was thinking of selling my sword and the horse. After listening to my story, she went to her room quietly and moments later came back and gave me ten Rupees. When I hesitated to take the money she said not to worry because she had made that money with a spinning wheel and that she had saved it for her funeral. She said that she was giving me an interest-free loan and that I could return it whenever I was able to do so.

"I took the money and after spending it on my way finally got to Odhaypour. There fortunately I got a job at the royal post. Quickly I was promoted and in short period of time because of good pay and free housing I was able to make and save money. After spending a few years there I got a letter from home that my eldest son was now old enough to marry and that his would be in-laws were insisting on an early wedding. I had to be there to fulfill my duty as a father.

"I applied for a leave and it was granted shortly thereafter and I left for home. When I reached Rewari, the memories of the old days flashed right before my eyes. When I reached the inn and asked about that prostitute, I was told that she was sick and dying. When I got to her room she was breathing her last and moments later died right before my eyes. I arranged for her funeral and took her lifeless body to the grave myself. On returning from the funeral I went to the motel and slept. At midnight, I realized that my wallet, which had a draft of five thousand rupees, was missing. I looked for it but could not find it. Then I realized that I must have dropped it when I was loading her body in the grave. I went to the cemetery in the middle of the night and opened her grave.

"When I entered the grave to my astonishment there was neither the body nor the wallet that had my draft. However, I had not seen a door there earlier. It was slightly open. I gathered enough courage to open it but there was a different world inside. On all sides, there were gardens and lush greenery. In the middle there was a magnificent palace. When I entered the palace I saw an extremely beautiful woman. She was dressed up in regal outfit with makeup and there were servants around her. She addressed me and said, 'You didn't recognize me? I am the one who gave you ten rupees. God liked my gesture and rewarded me with this glory and status. This is your wallet that fell in the grave. Take it and leave immediately.'

"I said I wanted to see her garden for a while. That beautiful woman said I would not be able to see it entirely even if I stayed there until Day of Judgment. She said, 'Leave immediately, you have no idea how far ahead the world must have gone by now.' I followed her advice and left the grave. Now there was neither the inn nor the tent nor that old township. Instead, a new city had sprung around it. When I asked some people about the inn, they were all unaware of it. When I told my story to some people they thought I was crazy. Eventually one of the people told me that he would take me to an old person who might know something about it. After listening to my story and after a brief pause he told me that his grandfather had told that some time ago there used to be an inn there. One night, a rich man had stayed in it and then mysteriously vanished. No one ever saw him or heard anything about him. I then told him that I was that rich man. After listening to me, the old man and his company were all taken aback."

After relating this story the rich man asked Hadrat Shah Abdul Aziz, "Please tell me what I should do now, where I should go. I have no home, no family. This whole event has crippled me."

Shah Sahib then said, "What you have seen is true. The scale of measurement of time in our world and that world is different." He then advised that man, "Go to Mecca and spend your remaining days in the remembrance of God."

27

Dress of Soul

It is generally thought that the skeletal structure of bones and flesh is what Man is though all the religious scriptures stress that it is not so. This body of bones and flesh is merely a dress for the soul. When the soul ends its attachment to its dress then the dress itself becomes of no value. You can burn it (cremation), mutilate it, or dump it in the ground (grave); it would not be able to resist any of it.

It is the eternal nature of the soul that it adopts a new body in every New World. Just as in this world it forms the body of bones and flesh, similarly in the life after death (*aeraaf*) it adopts a new body that has all the qualities and abilities that had existed before death. Over there (*aeraaf*) people do recognize one another and are aware of what happiness and sadness is. These people do distinguish those who are bound for hell from those who will eventually go to heaven.

> "And the people of Heaven called on the people of Fire that we receive what was promised to us by our Lord. Verily, didst thou get anything that was promised by thy Lord? And verily they said yea. Then a caller called down on them that curse of God to the unjust who shun the way of God and look for fault in it and deny the Day of Judgment."

Between these groups, there will be a wall separating them. At its peak (*aeraaf*) there will be some other people. They will recognize one another by the attire and will address the people of heaven thus: "Peace to thee..." These people had not yet entered the Heaven but will hope for it. When their sight fall on the people of Hell then they will say,"O'our Lord, please do not include us among these unjust." Then these people of *aeraaf* will address the prominent figures of Hell:

> "So thou finally seest, today neither thy wealth nor thy material goods which thou hast considered prominent is of any use. And are not the people of Heaven those for

whom thou used to swear that God will not give them any of His blessings. Today they are told to enter Heaven. Thou art not, but will know only fear and grief." [*Sura* Aeraaf: *Qur'an* (Koran)]

According to these verses of the *Qur'an* (Koran), after death souls of deceased formed into two groups, Alleen (upper) and Sajjeen (lower). This was described in the following verse,

"And what thou knowest, what *Sajjeen* is, it is in the Book of Record (Kitaab al-Marqoom)."
[*Sura* Mutafeen: 8-9]

"And what thou knowest, what Alleen is, it is in the Book of Records (Kitaab al-Marqoom)."
[*Sura* Mutafeen: 19-20]

This *Kitaab al-Marqoom* is the Book of Records that logs everything that humans do in this world during their lifetime in the form of a film (movie). Here we must point out that every thought, every imagination, every movement and action has a figure. Whatever we do becomes a film within the boundary of our own knowledge.

According to many religions, the punishment for murder is execution. Let us assume hypothetically that we commit a murder. First, the film would record our intention that we are planning a murder. Then we are going towards the place to commit the murder will be recorded. Then the act will also be recorded. Our reaction and our awareness that the punishment for murder is execution will be recorded too. The whole film will show first that John Doe leaves his home, kills so-and-so, is arrested, tried, and because of this is executed.

In the same way, every action is being recorded. After the death John Doe, the deceased, will behold that film; in other words, under a special program he will have to watch that film. At this level, John Doe will go through two states. First, he will forget that he is watching a film, and from here if he sees any pain he will feel it as well. The same way when we see a movie in theater or at home, so we respond to whatever is shown on the screen. If it is a comedy then we laugh and giggle, but if it is a movie about a tragedy then we unconsciously get mushy. On the other hand, a horror movie scares the devil out of out us.

The second state the deceased goes through while watching that film is that he becomes aware what lies ahead for him as result of what he did. He also goes through the guilt that he could have lived without committing those crimes whether it was murder, stealing, bribery or whatever. Besides, those for whom he committed those crimes are no longer in a position to help him.

A capitalist and greedy lover of wealth will see his film showing him usurping other people rights and money. And because of that people are hungry, worried, and deprived of essentials. Because of poverty, their own existence is a burden on them. Because he is the one who has total control over the resources. He will see that because of his greed people are suffering, they are hungry and destitute. And then he will realize that he is the one responsible for that suffering. Justice will be served when he goes through the same affliction they went through. The moment he realizes that he will see himself in the film being poor, destitute, worried, and anxious he will scream and cry but will find no one sympathetic to him.

28

Haatif Ghaybi

The universe has a collective consciousness. Every piece of sand, stars, satellites, animals, birds, insects, humans, ginns and angels receive the feedback of life from a consciousness which contains the absolute knowledge of the whole universe. In modern times we can use the analogy of a computer that has all the information loaded into it.

Through Muraqaba we are able to access that consciousness. One of the sources of communication with that consciousness is sound. This sound is known in Sufism as *Haatif e Gaybi*, which simply means the voice of the unseen world. This voice runs through the universe all the time. Anyone who can achieve higher mental concentration and is free of negative thoughts can not only hear it but can even get answers to questions.

In the universe, sound is what first and foremost that emerges. In the human senses, the hearing is first to register. When hearing is activated then the sight is able to focus on any given point. After that, the senses of touch and taste develop. At this level, the circle is completed. In other words, whatever man sees and feels are the extended features of the sound.

According to the *Qur'an* (Koran), in the beginning the sound of "KUN"(to be) emerged and the universe with its intricate detail came into being. However, at that moment the creatures had not come into their senses. The Creator addressed the created,

"Am I not your Lord?"

This voice gave the created ones the vision and the visionary senses were activated. With that, other senses followed. The created recognized the Divine after witnessing and realizing.

All religions stress the importance of sound. It is stated in the Gospel (*Injeel*),

"God said, let there be light and there was light."

145

In Hinduism, the sound of "Om" is considered the holiest of the holy. Hindu mystics believe that whatever exists between the cosmos (*akaash*) and the world (*dharty*) is the resonance of Om. According to them, a single voice runs in the entire universe continuously. They called it *Akaash Waany* (cosmic sound). Sufis also mention a hidden sound, which is referred as *Sauté Sarmadi* (Divine Voice). Through this voice, the Sufi Saints receive the intuitive guidance.

The correct method for listening to the *Haatif e Gaybi* is as follows:

1. Sit in the meditation style and put cotton balls in your ear.
2. Then turn the focus to your inner self and imagine a sound of one of the following.
3. Sweet melody of ringing bells.
4. The humming of honeybees.
5. The sound of the waterfalls. As when the water hits the ground.
6. Sound of flute.

When the student is able to maintain his or her focus, then eventually that sound becomes gradually audible. In the beginning, it comes in many forms and styles. Gradually words and sentences are audible in that sound as well. Through that voice, mysteries and secrets are revealed to the *muraqib* (student). Hidden events are foreseen and the line of communication is established from above. When the student has achieved excellence in this Muraqaba, he or she is able to converse with that voice and ask questions.

The correct method of asking questions with the *Haatif Ghaybi*:

When someone achieves the level where they can hear the *Haatif e Gaybi*, then involuntarily they receive the skill to ask questions and get answers. However, the correct method is as follows:

Repeat your question once or twice, then sit in a Muraqaba position, and turn your focus towards *Haatif e Gaybi* and maintain that focus. Now stop repeating your question and focus only on the *Haatif e Gaybi*. Relative to mental focus and strength, the students get their answers shortly in their mind.

TAFHEEM (Wisdom):

The Divine Name of *al-Aleem* is significant. Aleem means one who possesses knowledge and through its source all branches of knowledge are transferred to humans. The base of all branches of knowledge is the knowledge of the Divine Names (*isma elahiya*). Its first and foremost display is called *Tadjalli* (Divine Light)*. *Tadjalli* is *in fact* a mark, which contains within itself form and figure as well as movement. All the *tadjallis* of these Divine Names (*isma husna*) or attributes (*sifaat elahiya*) are marked inside the human spirit (*ruh*). These marks are in fact a record or file. Just like any microfiche, human spirit contains all the marks of the Divine Names *(isma elahiya).*

When a person is able to activate the link of the Divine Name, *al-Aleem*, then they are able to watch the *Tadjalli* of all the Divine Names (*isma husna*). This *nisbat* serves as a memory. Anyone trying to read that link during Muraqaba can do so during the stages of *idraak, varood* or *shahood.*

The way the Prophets of God and His saints have access to that memory or stored information is known in Sufism as *Tarze Tafheem* (Cognitive Mode). It is also referred as *Sayr* or *Fatah*. The literal meaning of *tafheem* is to gain understanding through awareness or to awaken it. From here through its Muraqaba, the knowledge of Divine Names (*ilm Ladani*) and those creative formulas are revealed which is the basis of the creation of this universe.

The Muraqaba of *Tafheem* is done past midnight. The student tries to concentrate on the Divine Name *al-Aleem* after emptying all the thoughts and imagining that he or she has the connective link of the Divine Name *al-Aleem*. During the learning period of *al-Aleem* the duration of wakefulness is increased besides practicing the Muraqaba. During *Tarze Tafheem*, the maximum time allowed for sleeping should not exceed two and a half hours in any twenty-four hour period. By being awake most of the time the Divine Name *al-Aleem* is fully activated with all of its energy. In the beginning most of the observation is witnessed when the eyes are closed during Muraqaba. However, later it happens while the eyes are open. When the vision appears with eyes closed it is referred as *Varood*, but when it happens with open eyes, it is called *Shahood.*

SPIRITUAL JOURNEY:

With continued Muraqaba and through the attentive care of the spiritual master, the Divine light stored inside the student is raised. This results in clearing the mirror of consciousness. When this stage arrives the student embarks on a never-ending spiritual journey. This journey has two stages. In the first stage, he or she witnesses the events as if they were distant. Until he or she reaches the Divine Throne (*arsh elahii*) and receives the *Tadjalli* of the Divine Characteristic (*sifaat elahiya*). This style of observation is known in Sufism as *Sayr Afaaq*(Heaven's Journey).

When this journey is completed and the student receives God's enlightenment, then the journey of Inner (*infas*) starts. At this stage the observation and revelation reveals in such a way that the student sees the entire cosmos in his or her Point of Essence (*nuqta dhat*) and the outward appears within. Sufis called this style of observation *Sayr Anfas* (Journey of Self). At the height of this level, the Gnostic (*arif*) sees God beyond the Divine Throne in the form of *Tadjalli*. The following two verses of the *Qur'an* (Koran) points to the *Sayr Anfas*:

"And He lives in your *nafs*, couldn't you see?"   "Soon We will show them our signs in *Anfas* and in *Afaaq*, until the Truth is revealed to them." (Chapter25 verse1)

When someone reaches the level where his or her inner vision is activated then they are given the Muraqaba to imagine the entire cosmos is a mirror in which the Divine Lights are being reflected. Through this imagination, *Sayr Afaaqi* begins. In the later stage, the student is given the Muraqaba to imagine that they themselves are mirrors in which the Divine Light and attributes are shining. This imagination begins the *Sayr Anfas*. At the height of this journey or stage, the mirror within is also negated so as to access the Divine Essence (*dhat elahii*).

There is another method in which the student imagines a bond and connection existing between his or her heart and the Divine Throne. From here, the student gradually reaches the Divine Throne. In the next stage he or she during Muraqaba and otherwise imagines these verses of the *Qur'an* (Koran) covering thems:

"He liveth with thee, wherever thou art"
"He is closer to your vein."
"He is inside your *Nafs*, Can't you see?"

MURAQABA OF HEART (*qalb*)

According to Sufism, the universe is like a circle *(chakra)* in a dimension, meaning that everything that exists in this universe is contained in a circle *(chakra)*. This enclosure of the cosmos in a single *circle (chakra)* is like a microfiche that contains all the pictures and facts in a small space. In the same sense, in this cosmic circle *(chakra)* all that exists is marked or contained. When this *circle (chakra)* activates, it extends into the outward universe. The other analogy would be that of a seed of a tree. That tiny seed, which is nothing but a circle, contains its entire history, leaves, flowers, fruits, branches and the future generation of that tree. That same seed eventually becomes the tree. In Sufism, that circle that contains the entire cosmos is referred as *qalb* (heart), *fawwad*, or *nafs vahida*.

The method of entering the depth of that circle *(chakra)* through Muraqaba of Heart is as follows:

By following the directions of your spiritual master (murshid) close your eyes and look inside your heart and through the imaginative vision, see that there is a black circle *(chakra)* in your heart. After some time the image will form. At that point, let your mind enter the depth of that circle *(chakra)*. What you see inside the realm of that circle *(chakra)* is proportional to the depth that occurs.

MURAQABA OF UNITY (*tawheed*)

When we study any movement occurring in the universe, we find they all have rhythm, a certain discipline. Because of that cosmic discipline, all relative functions are well organized also. For example a child is born in a fixed proportion and structure and then with a fixed timetable grows into an adolescent, then an adult and then into old age. Plants and other creatures are also living with fixed formulas. Every movement of stars and satellites is dependent on the specific system of gravity. The number of stars that are destroyed is almost the same as the new ones that are created. Nature takes care of all the needs of the creatures before after their birth. Water converts into vapors that form clouds in the atmosphere and the same clouds unload all that moisture in the form of rain. This water is essential for preserving life. The extra water that falls during rainfall is either absorbed by the land or is added to the bayous and river and eventually flows into the ocean.

These examples show there is an order in the Universe. The true reason for that is the single mind or unit that is behind this control. Through this mind all the units of the universe are functioning. This reality is called the Unity of Works (*tawheed if'aali*). This means there is a unity that exists in all the roles.

On whomever the Unity of Works is revealed, he or she is able to watch that behind the luminary world there exists a being, which is the controlling authority of the hidden world. The shadow of that hidden world is this universe. That person is able to see the relativity of one movement with the other. Meaning the person becomes aware of the relationship of two different movements. He or she can relate the source of any movement with the mind that is controlling the universe.

During the Muraqaba of Unity, the student imagines there is a unity in the cosmos. That unity is *in fact* a Light that is enveloping the entire universe.

MURAQABA OF NEGATION (*la*)

La in Arabic means no or negative. *La* is also the name of the lights emitting from one of the Divine Characteristics, a characteristic that we can analyze in humans. This characteristic is the unconscious. Usually unconscious is referred as the basis of those actions the human consciousness is unaware of. If we pay all of our attention to any on that basis with all of our mental strength that we could not understand or even when we grasp it, its meaning appears in our brain merely as a negative (*la*). Meaning we only regard it as negative.

Every rule of origin is the same, that is when we discuss or in our mind try to understand the origin of anything, the first thing that appear in the depth of our imagination is negation. In other words, in the beginning we are only aware of the void or nothingness.

When we get aware of anything even if it is the awareness of ignorance, it is awareness nevertheless. Every awareness is a reality. Therefore, we are bound to call the awareness of ignorance knowledge as well. In Sufism the awareness of ignorance is known as knowledge of "*la*" and the awarenace of knowledge is referred as knowledge of "*illa*".

The Divine lights of "*la*" are those Attributes of God that introduce us to the Oneness. After recognizing the Divine Lights of La the Gnostic's mind becomes fully aware of the concept of Oneness or Unity (*tawheed*). This is the first point through which a Sufi or Gnostic takes a step into the God-consciousness.

In the beginning of that step, he or she gets acquainted with his or her own self. Though after searching for themselves they could not get hold of it; which brings them to the correct awareness and realization of God consciousness (*ma'arifa*). This is the station which is commonly referred in Sufi text as '*fana* (annihilation).

Through the Muraqaba of *la* the mind becomes aware of the workings of the Saints, Khidr and Angels and is able to communicate with them. One ability of *La* is that it translates the meaning of the cryptic messages of Khidr, Saints of Takveen, and Angels into the language of the Gnostic into his or her hearing. Gradually a full line of communication is developed and with the help of Angels, numerous hidden affairs are revealed.

During the Muraqaba of "*la*" the eyes must be closed as much as possible. That is why a soft handkerchief or small towel is wrapped over the eyes to apply a little pressure to the eyes. During the Muraqaba the Gnostic puts the mind into the depth of his or her own self by moving away from all thoughts and imaginations. The aim is to achieve thoughtlessness by recognizing ignorance in their thought.

MURAQABA OF VOID

The Muraqaba of Void is the subbranch of the above mentioned Muraqaba. During this Muraqaba, the student imagines those conditions that reflect void or nothingness. His or her focus is the realm where there is nothing. No humankind, no trees, no animals and no sound. With no time and no space, they even feel themselves as nonexistent.

In the beginning it is quiet difficult to imagine. Because under normal circumstances no one goes through a condition in which there is a negation. Keeping this in mind, the Muraqaba of Void is given systematically. The idea is to familiarize the student first with the reflection of void instead of the total void. For example:

The student imagines a desert or empty plateau where there is total silence and everything is motionless. In Sufism this Muraqaba is also known as *Muraqaba Barri* (land).

The student imagines that in a wide ocean whose water is still, the student is immersed in it. This Muraqaba is known as Muraqaba Bahr(ocean). The student imagines that he or she no longer exists, only God is present.

These imaginations are not difficult to form and when these levels are passed then the Muraqaba of Void is given to practice.

Through the Muraqaba of Void, the student goes through the states which are contrary to the consciousness state of mind. When consciousness state becomes dormant then the subconscious state takes over. It is imperative to note that void does not mean a world where nothing exists; it simply means a world which can only be explored through the subconscious.

MURAQABA OF 'fana (ANNIHILATION):

When someone starts writing an essay the first thing that usually comes to his or her mind is the topic. At this point, the mind does not have the contents and details of that topic. However, when that person takes the pen (or keyboard) and activates the mind then the details of that essay start to form. Whatever he or she writes exists in their subconscious before. From that storage the contents take the form of words. In that essay, there is nothing that does not exist in that person's subconscious in the form of the content and meaning of the subject matter. If this did not exist then the essay would not have been able to take the form of words. Therefore, there are three stages in this writing process. The first stage is the one where the content of the essay exists in unwritten form; the second, where it is transformed into words; and third, where the pen writes down those words on the paper and therefore gives it a material form.

Just as the essay has three forms and it takes three stages to reach its final stage, all outward phenomena exist in three spheres. Any existence or movement whether it belongs to past, present, or future is not outside these three spheres. This could further be explained by the example of an artist. This artist makes a painting of an eagle on a canvas. If he wants to paint another painting of the same bird, he can. The reason is because the forms and figure of eagle is stored in his mind. What displays on the canvas is merely a reflection of that. The picture does not. He can make as many paintings as he wants; however, the knowledge of that bird never leaves his mind.

Any knowledge, any movement, any phenomenon wherever it exists in the meaningful form is called the Realm of Allegory (*a'lam mithaal*). In this realm, every display consists of form and figure, which is visible to the spiritual eye. When a man tries to learn these figures through Muraqaba then his consciousness is able to gain knowledge of these figures. In these figures lies the event of the future, which shows according to their schedule.

To learn the Realm of Allegory, Muraqaba of '*fana* is given:

The student after closing his or her eyes imagines that all the signs of their life are wiped out and there exists only in the form of a point of light. They try to force the idea into their mind that they are free from their self and are now connected only with the world whose boundary contains the events from the beginning of time (*a'zal*) to the end-time(*ab'ed*).

The more a person practices the Muraqaba the deeper the reflection of the Realm of Allegory is revealed to his or her mind. Gradually its meaning is also transferred into their consciousness.

MURAQABA, DIVINE NAMES

When we discuss something or someone, we describe its characteristics. Without describing the attributes, it is not possible to explain anything that exists. The collection of certain characteristics is what we call a thing. When we describe the material forms, we say whether it is solid or liquid or gas. A certain color is dominant in it. So-and-so chemicals are part of it, whether that thing is round or square or of any other shape.

Everything is given a name and it is the name alone that represents a particular characteristic of any given thing. For example, when we say water, we mean that liquid that is used to quench the thirst. However, we know that it can be used for other purposes as well.

When we say water then the person hearing that word recognizes the characteristic or the meaning of water. Therefore when we say pen, we mean the thing that is used for writing. This suggests the collection of attributes (*sifaat*) is usually shown as a symbol. This symbol can be given a name. According to Sufism the Universe is the collection of the attributes. The common organization of the attributes is responsible for creation. Spiritualists have viewed the attributes in the depth of creation and have given them various names.

Prophets of God received the knowledge of attributes through revelation (*vahi*). According to them the characteristics that are functional in this universe are the Divine Attributes (*sifaat e'lahiya*). The difference is that these characterics exists in the Divine Essence (*dhat*) in their entirety and the created forms have only gotten part of it. For example, God has sight, meaning that vision is characteristic of God and the created have also vision. God can hear and so does the creation. God has said that among the creators He is the best creator. On the other hand, that God is more merciful than any other. is. In other words, any characteristic that God has is not only supreme in quality but also limitless, whereas creatures have those same characteristic in a limited fashion.

NAME OF DIVINE ESSENCE (*dhat*)

The Divine name of Essence (*dhat*) meaning Al-Lah has a special significance. That is why Sufis recommend Muraqaba of the Name of Essence in order to create a link and to watch the divine Light of that name.

This whole universe is based on the fact that it belongs to a single Being, meaning He is the only Lord of all the creatures. Due to this Reality all creatures are aware of one another and are in the service to one another. If this universe had not belonged to a single Being, then there would not have been any link between the creatures. This Lord of the Universe is called Al-Lah and in the Divine Names this is the Name of Essence. Other names show the Divine Attributes. In the name of Al-Lah a certain Light is hidden which reveals the creativeness and the sovereignty. Through this Light, a person is able to see the foundation of the Universe, because creativity and sovereignty are extended to all the creatures.

In the Muraqaba the students imagine that in their heart the Name of Essence Al-Lah is written in luminary letters and its rays are all over the body of that student. Therefore the deeper the imagination is formed, the higher the Gnostic sees the entire cosmos immersed in the light of Divine Name of Essence. At its height, God's characteristic of Creation and Sovereignty is revealed in his heart.

29

Tassawar Shaykh

This Universe is a collection of all those planets, stars, humans, animals, and all the other living beings. There is a link between all the creatures in this cosmos. Whether the physical eyes see that link or not we can not help but attest to its existence.

When we look at anything, the first thing we do is to see it. By beholding it, we get the idea of its essence and its characteristics. Similarly when we think, see, or hear about any particular thing then its essence and attributes flow into us. When we see fire, or imagine it or discuss it, then the attributes of fire flow within us in the form of perception. Whether this process is very low or high to the point of feeling is another matter, but it does happen. With the imagination of fire, we sense heat and light. In the same way, just by hearing about a lush green place (for instance, Hawaii), a sense of calm and serenity overcomes us.

Based on this rule when we see John Doe or hear about him, then what appears in our mind is not his name or its spelling, instead what appears is his image and personality, which is a collection of unlimited attributes.

There are two ways by which knowledge or skill can be transferred to humans. First, he or she has to gradually learn any branch of knowledge or skill, one step at a time. The teacher by ways of words, written manuals, or demonstration, instills that particular skill or knowledge in the student. The student on the other hand gradually absorbs the content of what is taught over a period. Depending on the depth of the knowledge and the learning ability and enthusiasm of the student the whole process may stretch to weeks, months, or even years.

In the second way of learning, words, writing or demonstration is not needed. Knowledge or skill is simply transferred based on the concentration and mental coherence itself. The best example of this type of learning is the learning of the Native language. The child does not take any written or spoken lessons from his mother or those other people from his environment. Yet merely because of creative cohesiveness and mental nearness and link, he begins to speak the language of his mother or of the people of his environment. He draws the same meaning from the words, and sentences of the language the way other people do. Not only the native language but also many other skills and habits are transferred to the child from his environment as well. The child does not have to go through the usual role of a student.

In the spiritual sciences, the transfer of knowledge is carried out using the later method. Through this spiritual link between the Master (*shaykh*) and the student (*murid*), the angle of perception and the light of knowledge is gradually transferred to the student until he is able to grasp the true meaning of the subject matter. Secondarily the Spiritual Master teaches the spiritual knowledge through different grades, lessons, and demonstrations as well so the consciousness of the student would be able to retain it in an orderly fashion.

The love (*ishq*) for the Spiritual Master also serves as the tonic for the mind of the student. As the student joins the company of the Master, asks questions, and learns from the directions (*irshad*) of the Master, then based on the above mentioned Creative Rule, the personality and qualities of the Master start flowing into the inner self of the student (*murid*). That is why being often in the company of the Spiritual Master is always strongly encouraged.

The other aspect of this Rule is for the student to use that power of imagination to absorb the qualities of the Master. To carry it out, the Muraqaba of the imagination of the Master (*shaykh*) is given, so that through the imagination a mental link can flourish with the Master. Therefore, when a student imagines his or her Spiritual Master, then his qualities and skills start flowing in their soul. The longer the focus the more the attributes and his light of knowledge fall on the mental screen of the student. Continued practice of the imagination of the Master creates a state in which the spiritual link with the Master is established permanently. Through this link the capacity of Divine Cognizance is gained as well until a point is reached when the student (*murid*) becomes the reflection of his Master (*muraad*). In Sufism, this station is referred as *'fana fi shaykh* and the imagination of the Master itself as *tassawar shaykh*.

There are different methods in use:

The student imagines during the Muraqaba that the Master is sitting in front of him. The student imagines the Master is focusing on him and the lights (*anwaar*) and blessings (*barakah*) are being absorbed into him. The essence of the Master is enveloping him. He sees himself as the personification of his Master as though his essence is the same as of his Master. This is best of all the methods as in it the student negates his own self or ego.

30

Tassawar Rasul

It is imperative for a qualified Sufi Master to have gained the spiritual link (*nisbat*) with the Prophet Muhammad and have gained his perceptivity (*tarz-e-fikr*).

When a student achieves *"fana fi shaykh"* (as described in chapter-29) then his perceptivity and traits of personality mirror those of his Spiritual Master (*shaykh*) and he starts to assimilate the essence of the Prophet Muhammad. To improve this link, the student is given the Muraqaba of *tasawwar rasul* (visualization of the Prophet) so their spiritual connection improve and they could receive the blessings of the Light of Prophethood (*nur nabu'wat*). Depending on the prophet Muhammad's intercession, the students see the Light of Prophethood based on their ability, which is subject to his approval. When the Light of Prophethood fills the inner self of the students, they achieve the station of *"fana fi rasul."*

There are different methods of *tassawar rasul*:

In the Muraqaba, the student imagines the Mosque of Medina (*masjid nabawi*) or its green dome. The students imagine the lights from the city of Medina are being absorbed in their inner. In the heart of the student, the word Muhammad is written in luminescent form and his heart lit because of it. The Prophet Muhammad is sitting in the crown of Prophethood and from his heart the lights are falling into the student's heart. The student imagines that he or she is sitting with the Prophet and that he is watching them.

Just as Muslims consider the Prophet Muhammad to be their mediator or medium to God, members of other faiths consider other personalities to be their medium between them and God. Jews regard Moses as such while Christian mystics consider Jesus, Hindus consider Krishna or Ram, and Zoroastrians consider Zoroaster to be their medium. Buddhists believe in redemption through Buddha. Based on this belief, in these religions the Muraqaba of these personalities is given after the Muraqaba of the *guru*.

31
Divine Essence

The mind of the Prophet Muhammad, on which *tadjalli* constantly falls, is directly linked to the Divine. When a seeker of the Truth is able to form a spiritual closeness with the Prophet to an extent such that his or her mind fills with the blessings and the Lights of Prohethood (*nur nabuwat*), then the *tadjalli* of God begins descending on them. In order to strenghten this ability Muraqaba of Divine Essence (*al dhat e'lahiya*) is given to practice so that the link could be established and deepen and the journey of Gnosis of Essence (*irfan e'lahiya*) could go on forever. When the person achieves the desired concentration on the *tadjalli* of Divine Essence, then this stage is called *'fana fi Al-Lah* or *'fana fi dhat* (annihilation into the Divine).

In this Muraqaba, instead of the Attributes the Essence is imagined. The Divine Essence is beyound words and could not be explained. No flight of human consciousness could ever reach its furthest boundaries; however, within the limits of perception, God can be felt.

It is stated in the *Qur'an* (Koran):

> "And no man could ever be able to converse with Him; unless through signs, or behind the veil or through a messenger" [*Sura* Shura:51].

The above verse sheds some light on the reach of human senses. When God addresses humans, He uses signs and the heart is able to see and recognize. This divine way of communication is called *vahii*. In the second method God sends a messenger (angel) and the human eye is able to see the messenger. In the third way God reveals a glimpse of Himself to His servant (man). This is known as *hijab* (Divine Veil). In this way God reveals Himself in a beautiful and luminous (*nur a'la nur*) face. This beautiful face is not God but His Veil.

In the Muraqaba of visualization of the Essence (*al dhat*) God is approached through different methods of dialogue. There are various types of this Muraqaba.

1. The student visualizes that in his heart the Divine Name Al-Lah is written in a luminous way and through its light the entire cosmos brightens.

2. That he is prostrating before Him at the Divine Throne (*arsh*).

3. The Divine Essence is before him in the form of *tadjalli*.

4. God is focused on him and this focus is in the form of lights shining on the student.

5. The student visualizes that God is beholding him. This is known as the Muraqaba of *royet*.

6. It is stated in the *Qur'an* (Koran),

> "Wherever thou art, God is with thee." Hence in the Muraqaba the omnipresence of God is visualized. This is known as Muraqaba of *ma'eeyet* (company).

7. In the Muraqaba the following verse of the *Qur'an* (Koran) is visualized,
> "We are closer to thee than thy cardinal vein."

This Muraqaba is called the Muraqaba of *aqrab*.

8. "Wherever thou facest, thou seest God." Based on this verse, the student visualizes that God is everywhere.

9. It is stated in the *Qur'an* (Koran) that, "God is encircling everything that exists." Hence the student visualizes that God is enveloping the entire cosmos.

10. In the Muraqaba the God is visualized as an endless Sea in which the student is like a tiny drop immersed in it.

11. It is visualized that the entire Universe is annihilated and the only Being that exists is God.

When the student gains excellence in these types of Muraqaba then with the help of his Spiritual Master and the grace of the Prophet Muhammad, he witnesses the *tadjalli* of the Divine Essence.

Glossary

Adab: Protocol. Etiquette, Respect.

Ahlul Bayt: The Quranic (Koranic) term for the immediate family of Prophet Muhammad. Usually meant for Prophet Muhammad, His daughter Fatima Zehra, Her husband Imam Ali and their two sons Imam Hasan al-Mujtaba and Imam Husayn Shaheed Kerbala.

Al-Lah: Arabic term for God.

A'lam akbar: Macrocasm. Cosmos. Universe.

A'lam asghar: Microcasm. Man.

A'lam al-ghayb: the Unseen realm.

Arsh: Divine Throne.

Baqa: Survival. This stage come after fana, when the Gnostic return to his or her improved Self after being absorbed in God.

Batin: Esoteric or mystical meaning of the Qur'an. Inward religion or tradition.

Dargah: Sufi Shrine.

Dervish: Sufi, Sufi student, Sufi-like, monk. The term generally used in Turkish influenced areas like Balkans, Turkey, Central Asia and Iran. For example the whirling dervish of the Mawlawiyyah Sufi Order.

Dhikr: Remembrance of God prescribed in the Qur'an. In Sufism, dhikr is done by reciting a selected Divine Name by tongue or by heart as a mantra. For example in the Sufi Order of Azeemia, Ya-Hayiu Ya-Qayumu is given for dhikr.

Fana: Annihilation. Complete surrender of the Self to the Divine. Self-negation.

Faqir: also fakir. lit., Destitute, poor. A wandering Sufi monk.

Farsi: Persian.

Fatah: Revelation. In Sufism, a state in which the student is able to see the unseen.

Fiqh: Islamic jurisprudence.

Ghauth-Pak: Title of Shaykh Abdul Qadir Jilani, founder of Quadiriya Order.

Hadith: sayings of the Prophet Muhammad.

Iblis: Satan. According to Qur'an, when God ordered angels to prostrate before Adam, all did except Iblis, who insisted on his superiority over Adam. Thus, he was condemned and thrown out of the Divine Court. When confronted by God, Iblis refused to take any responsibility and accused God of straying him. Also, persuaded Eve to taste the forbidden tree.

Ihsan: A state of awareness in which a person feels as if they are watching God or God is watching them constantly. Also known as martaba-e-ihsan.

Ilm, ilm ladani: According to Sufism, Primordial Knowledge given to Adam and after him given to all the prophets and apostles of God. After the closure of prophethood, the knowledge was transferred through Imam Ali and his descendents to other Sufi Saints. The ultimate reward for any Sufi.

Imam: lit. leader. In Sunni Islam term applies to anyone who leads prayers. However, in Shi'i Islam and in Sufism, the term used for the descendents of Prophet Muhammad through his daughter Fatima and son-in-law Imam Ali.

Injeel: Gospel. The first four books of the New Testament.

Ishq: Spiritual, selfless love (verses hu'b= love that longs for physical contact, aqeedat=devotional love that relies on imitation).

Jalal: Divine Majesty.

Jamal: Beauty.

Jinn: According to Qur'an, an unseen creature other than angels or humans.

Jadhab: Absorbtion. Permanet surrender of the conscious to the Divine.

Jazb: see jadhab.

Jesus: Prophet Isa ibn Maryam.

John the Baptist: Prophet Yahya.

Joseph: Prophet Yusuf.

Kaaba: the Grand Mosque in Mecca. Said to have been first built by Abraham with Ishmael at his side.

Karamat: Miracles performed by Sufi saints.

Kashaf: Spiritual vision.

Kashaf ul Qaboor: Revelation of the life after death.

Khalifa: In Sufism. A person who has received the ilm from his Shaykh. Also used to denote successor of a Shaykh.

Khanqah: Sufi convent.

Khilafat: In Sunni and Shi'i Islam simply a secular or theocratic leadership. However, in Sufism the term is used for that ilm or knowledge that once God bestowed it to Adam, He ordered all angels to prostrate before Adam. Also known as ilm ladani, ilm al-asma.

Lungar: Free meal offered at Sufi shrines.

Majdhoub: one who has surrendered his conscious to the Divine, permanently. Holy mad-man.

Majzoob: see majdhoub.

Moses: Prophet Musa.

Murad: Shaykh, Sufi Master.

Muraqaba: Meditation. Contemplation.

Muraqib: One who is in the state of Muraqaba.

Murid: Disciple, student. One who is initiated into a Sufi Order.

Murshid: Sufi Master.

Nafs: Soul.

Nafs al-ammarah: see ruh-e-hevani.

Nafs al-lawwama: see ruh-e-insani.

Nafs al-mutmain'na: see ruh-e-azam.

Nur: Invisible pure light.

Pak-Punjtain: lit.,The Holy Five. See Ahlul Bayt.

Pir: Sufi Master.

Qalandar: A high-ranking Sufi, who has overcome the restriction of Time and Space.

Qawwali: Spiritual music performed primarily in Sufi shrines. Also known as sa'ma.

Qutb: A high-ranking Sufi.

Ruh: Spirit. Soul.

Ruh-e-azam: Higher Self, Contented Soul. According to Sufism, this soul carries the primordial knowledge.

Ruh-e-insani: Ego. Intellect.

Ruh-e-hevani: Lower Self.

Sa'ma: Spiritual music.

Shahood: a level of Sufi learning, where the student is able to observe beyond the limits of Time and Space.

Shaykh: Sufi Master.

Shia: One of the two major outward legalistic traditions of Islam. See Sunni.

Silsila: lit., chain. Sufi Order. Tariqa.

Sufi, Sufism: the esoteric and mystical version of Islam. Islamic Gnosis.

Sunni: One of the two major outward legalistic tradition of Islam. See Shia.

Tariqa: Sufi Order.

Tassawuf: original term for Sufism.

Tekke: Sufi convent primarily in Turkish areas.

Torah: the first five books of the Old Testament given to Moses.

Urdu: Indo-European language of Turkish origin. Lingua franca of Pakistan, India, Nepal, Dubai. Widely used in Mauritius and Suriname. Written in Arabic script.

Urs: lit. Wedding. Passing away of the Sufi Saint, thus a union with God, the Beloved. Also used for the death anniversary of the saint, which is usually a time of celebration for the devotees.

Va'da-e-Alust: When God created souls out of non-existence, they were initially in a state of bewilderment. Then God addressed them, Am I not (alust) your Lord, the beings collectively replied bala (Yea) we testify. This event is mentioned in Qur'an and is known in the Sufi literature as the Vada-e-Alust (Covenant of Alust). By testifying together, creatures gained collective conscious.

Wahabi: a militant, intolerant, extremist sect of Saudi origin. Denies existence of Spirituality in Islam. Also known as Salafi (North Africa), Ahl-e-Hadith (Pakistan).

Zaboor: Psalms. Book of David.

Zikr: see dhikr.

Suggested Reading

✓Ali, Imam. *Nahjul Balagha* (Peak of Eloquence). Sayings, letters and sermons of Imam Ali ibn abi Talib, compiled by 7th century A.D. scholar Allama Syed Muhammad Razi.

Arabi, ibn. *Futuhat makkiyah* (The Meccan Revelation).

Armstrong, Karen. *History of God*. New York, Ballantine Books,1993.

_____, *Muhammad, A Biography of the Prophet*. San Francisco, HarperCollins,1992.

✓Attar, Fariduddin. *Memoirs of the Saints*. trans. by Bankey Behari. Lahore, Pakistan: Sh. Muhammad Ashraf, 1965.

Awliya, Qalandar Baba. *Rubaiyat* (Urdu, poetry). Karachi, Al-Kitaab Publications.

_____, *Loh-o-Qalam*, (Urdu) Essays on Spirituality. Karachi, Maktaba-e-Tajuddin Baba, 1978.

Azeemi, Khwaja Shamsuddin. *Avaz-e-Dost*. (Urdu) inspirational essays. Karachi, Maktaba-e-Roohani Digest,1996

_____, *Jannat ki Sayr*. (Urdu) anecdotes of spiritual encounters.Karachi. Al-Kitaab Publications, 1988.

_____, *Kashkoal*. (Urdu) inspirational essays. Lahore, Pakistan. Maktaba-e-Azeemia,1995.

_____, *Muhammad Rasul Al-Lah*, vol. I, II, III, IV (Urdu) anecdotal biography of the founder of Islam. Karachi, Al-Kitaab Publications, 1994.

_____,. *Parapsychology* (Urdu) Lectures on parapsychology. Karachi, Al-Kitaab Publications, 1985.

_____, *Qalandar sha'oor.* (Urdu) Karachi, al-Kitaab Publications, 1980.

_____, *Roohani Aelaaj.* (Urdu) Spiritual healing. Karachi, Maktaba Tajuddin Baba, 1983.

_____, *Roohani Namaz.* (Urdu). Karachi, Maktaba Tajuddin Baba, 1984.

_____, *Rang aur Roshni say Aelaaj.* (Urdu) Spiritual healing based on color therapy. Karachi. Maktaba-e-Tajuddin Baba, 1987.

_____, *Tadjalliyat.* (Urdu) inspirational essays. Karachi, Maktaba-e-Roohani Digest, 1996.

_____, *Taujeehaat.* (Urdu) Lectures and articles of Shaykh Azeemi on Spirituality, compiled by Mian Mushtaq Ahmed Azeemi. Lahore, Pakistan. Maktaba-e-Azeemia 1994.

_____, *Tazkira-e-Qalandar Baba Awliya.* (Urdu) a short biography of the founder of the Sufi Order of Azeemia. Karachi, Maktaba-e-Tajuddin Baba, 1980.

. _____, *Telepathy seekhiyae* (Urdu) Self-help guide to learning Telepathy. Karachi, Al-Kitaab Publications, 1986.

Azeemi, Mian Mushtaq Ahmed. *Khanqahi Nizaam.* (Urdu) An introduction to several Sufi orders. Lahore, Pakistan. Maktaba-e-Azeemia, 1989.

_____, *Yaran-e-tariqat.* (Urdu) a short biography of Sufi saints. Lahore, Pakistan. Maktaba-e-Azeemia , 1988.

Azeemi, Monis Khan. *AllahRakkhi.* (Urdu/fiction) Lahore, Pakistan. Maktaba-e-Azeemia, 1988.

_____, *Pir Hazir Shah.* (Urdu/fiction) Lahore, Pakistan. Maktaba-e-Azeemia, 1986

_____, *Sada Suhagan Mastani.* (Urdu/fiction) Karachi, Maktaba-e-Roohani Digest, 1985.

Azeemi, Sohail. *Tazkira-e-Baba Tajuddin.* (Urdu) A short, anecdotal biography of the Indian Sufi Saint of Nagpur. Karachi, Maktaba-e-Tajuddin, 1983.

Azeemi, Syeda Saeeda Khatoon. *Andar ka Musafir.* (Urdu/fiction) Karachi, Al-Kitaab Publications, 1997.

✓Bawa Muhaiyadeen,M.R. *The Asma ul Husna: Ninety-Nine Beautiful Names.* Philadelphia, Fellowship Press, 1979.

Dyer, Wayne W. *The Power of Intention.* Carlsbad, Hay House USA, 2004.

_____, *10 Secrets for Success and Inner Peace.* Carlsbad, Hay House USA, 2001.

Ernst, Carl W. *Sufism: An essential introduction to the philosophy and practice of the mystical tradition of Islam.* Boston, Shambhala, 1997.

_____, *Following Muhammad: Rethinking Islam in the Contemporary World.* Chapel Hill, NC: University of North Carolina Press, 2003.

Frager, Robert. *Essential Sufism.* Co-editor James Fadiman San Francisco, HarperCollins, 1997.

Haeri, Shaykh Fadhlalla. *The elements of Sufism.* Boston, Elements Books,1990.

Hasan, Asma Gull. *Why I am a Muslim: An American Odyssey.* Boston, Elements Books,2004.

Heehs, Peter. *Indian Religions: A Historical Reader of Spiritual Expression and Experience.* New York, New York University Press,2002.

Helminski, Camille Adams. *Women of Sufism, A Hidden Treasure; Writings and stories of mystic poets, scholars and saints.* Boston, Shambhala, 2003.

✓Helminski, Kabir Edmund. *The Knowing Heart: A Sufi Path of Transformation.* Boston, Shambhala,2000.

Momen, Moojan. *An Introduction to Shi'i Islam: The History and Doctrines of Twelver Shi'ism.* New Haven, Yale University Press,1985.

Nasr, Seyyed Hossein. *Sufi Essays*. Albany: Suny Press, 1991.

Quadiri, Syed Fazl Kareem. *Maye Haqiqat Bajam-e-Shariat*. (Urdu) Karachi, 1979.

Redfield, James. *The Celestine Prophecy: An Adventure* (fiction). New York, Warner Books, 1993.

_____, *The Secrets of Shambhala: In Search of the Eleventh Insight* (fiction). New York, Warner Books, 1999.

Sadiq, Imam Ja'far al-. *The Lantern of the Path*. Shaftesbury, England: Elements Books, 1989.

Schimmel, Annemarie. *Mystical Dimensions of Islam*. Chapel Hill: University of North Carolina press, 1975.

Shah, Ghauth Ali. *Tazkira Ghauthya*.

Stepaniants, Marietta T. *Sufi Wisdom*. Albany, State University of New York, 1994.

Wolfe, Michael. *Taking Back Islam: American Muslims Reclaim Their Faith*. Rodale Books, 2004.

Index

A

a'alm akbar 2
a'lam al-ghayb ix, x, 85, 86, 159
a'lam asghar 1, 2, 46, 159
a'lam mithaal 152
aal-imran 43, 44
Aaron 49, 129
Abraham 48, 128, 160
Adam ix, 40, 96, 119, 160
Aeraaf 79, 86, 87, 129, 131, 138, 139, 142, 143
Afaaq 147, 148
Ahlul Bayt 43, 138
akaash 146
Akaash Waany 146
akhfa 33, 34
al dhat e'lahiya 157
al-Aleem 146, 147
alam al-mithal 54
alam khiyal 54
al-Baqara 44
al-dhat 51
al-ghayb ix, x, 85, 86, 88, 159
Al-Lah viii, 47, 48, 71, 74, 127, 129, 153, 157, 158, 159, 163
Ali, Imam x, 51, 160, 161, 163
al-nafs al- mutma'inna 33
al-nafs al-ammara 33
al-nafs al-lawwama 33
al-Qadeer 54
amr 30, 82
Anfas 148
angels 3, 12, 39, 48, 50, 68, 84, 85, 89, 90, 92, 93, 94, 95, 96, 130, 133, 134, 136, 145, 150, 160
anxiety 59, 60, 67, 112, 133, 138
arif 90, 148, 159

Arjuna 55
arsh 116, 126, 129, 147, 158
arsh elahii 147
asana 55
Aura 32, 78, 97, 131
Azeemia iii, xii, 63, 83, 159, 163, 164

B

Baba Ji 83, 85, 86
batin vii, 40, 42, 43, 45, 159
Benzene 10
Bhagavad Gita 55
BLUE LIGHT 115, 118, 119, 120
Book of Records 143
Buddha 55, 56, 156
Buddhism 55

C

cave of Hira 50, 51, 55
chakra 18, 33, 75, 92, 93, 94, 95, 148, 149
chemia sa'adat 48
Christianity 55
Christians xii, 45, 129
Cognitive Mode 147
Colorful Dreams 63
confusion 9, 59, 104, 105, 107, 108
conscience 9, 11, 34, 66, 93, 94, 138
Consciousness x, xi, 1, 5, 6, 7, 8, 10, 11, 14, 18, 20, 21, 22, 25, 26, 27, 28, 30, 31, 33, 37, 38, 39, 40, 45, 47, 48, 54, 55, 57, 58, 61, 62, 64, 75, 77, 78, 79, 80, 81, 82, 83, 85, 86, 93, 94, 101, 103, 104, 105, 108, 109, 110, 117, 131, 139, 145, 147, 150, 151, 152, 155, 157, 160, 161
contemplation vii, 42, 43, 45, 46, 53, 161

cosmic film 20

Cosmos 1, 2, 13, 37, 38, 46, 97, 146, 148, 149, 153, 154, 158, 159

D

Darood Sharif 129, 159

Day of Judgement 45

dhat 6, 22, 51, 52, 90, 148, 153, 157

dhat elahii 148

dhikr 43, 48, 51, 52, 53, 54, 63, 74, 76, 86, 116, 127, 159, 162

dhikr khaf I 54

dhikr lisani 54

dhikr qalbi 54

dhikr roohi 54

distress 18, 59, 134

Divine Attributes ix, 12, 47, 85, 90, 153

Divine Cognition 82

Divine Commandments 52

Divine Essence 43, 50, 51, 86, 148, 153, 157, 158

Divine Guidance 48, 104

Divine Help 73

Divine Knowledge 2, 23, 26, 72, 77, 83

Divine Laws 40, 90, 94, 129

Divine Light 30, 54, 80, 81, 82, 90, 125, 126, 146, 147, 148, 153

Divine Name ix, 48, 54, 116, 125, 146, 147, 153, 158, 159

Divine Names ix, 47, 54, 81, 82, 85, 86, 146, 147, 152, 153

Divine Revelation 40

Divine Throne 12, 116, 125, 126, 129, 130, 136, 147, 148, 158

Divine Unity 40, 41

Divine Veil 80, 82, 157

Divine Voice 146

Divine Will 30, 81, 82

Divine Wisdom 79, 82

Divine Word 82

Dome of the Rock 51, 77

drowsiness 17, 27, 33, 34, 62, 63, 75, 77, 99, 100

E

Ego vii, 24, 26, 33, 46, 131, 138, 155, 161

Enlightenment 56, 147

esoteric vision 8, 17, 77, 78, 102, 138

Eve 96, 160

Extra Sensory Perception 9, 11

Ezra 44

F

faidh 48, 70, 138

Fajr 76, 116, 126, 127

fana 150, 151, 152, 155, 157

fana fi rasul 156

fana fi shaykh 155, 156

fatah 91, 147, 159

fawwad 148

fikr vii, 43, 46, 52, 64, 156

fikr lateef 64

Freudian Psychology 25

G

Ga'yan 45

Gabriel 50, 80, 129

Gaya, India 56

Generators ix, 29, 30, 80

ghanood 34

Ghauth Ali Shah 47, 139

ghayb ix, x, 45, 85, 86, 88, 159

gnosis 42, 48, 52, 83, 157, 160, 161

Gnosis of Essence 157

GREEN LIGHT 122

H

Haatif Ghaybi 97, 145, 146

hadith 46, 47, 53, 131, 160, 162
hajj 51
haqiqat kubra 52
Heaven 12, 68, 93, 94, 96, 133, 139, 142, 143, 147
Hell 12, 94, 133, 142
hijab 157
hidaya 48
hijab ilahi 82
Hinduism 55, 137, 146
Holy Scriptures 82
hysteria 59, 123

I

Ibn Mubarak 47
idraak 75, 77, 147
ihsaan 42, 125, 126
ilhaam 27, 55, 78, 79, 80
ilm vii, ix, 26, 72, 147, 160
ilm ladani 26, 72, 147, 160
Imam Ghazali 48
iman 45
infas 147
injeel 50, 145, 160
inner dimensions 2, 46
inner plane 2, 7
inner self 2, 4, 8, 41, 76, 146, 155, 156
insomnia 59, 60
Intuitive ecstasy 33
irfan e'lahiya 157
Isaac 128
Islam 43, 45, 50, 53, 55, 160, 161, 162, 163, 165, 166
ism e'lahi 54
isma e'lahiya 82, 85, 146, 147
isma husna 147
iss'fal 107
istaghraaq 110, 112, 113

J

jabal al musa 49
Jacob 128

Jannat Ki Sayr 92, 163
jaundice 59
Jerusalem 44, 49, 51, 77
Jesus 40, 49, 50, 55, 156, 160
Jews 45, 129, 156
jinns 12, 39, 45, 63
jism mithali 32
John the Baptist 49, 160
Joseph 26, 160
Jot 137
Judaism 55

K

Kaaba 69, 85, 89, 160
Kalima Shahada 129
Karachi xii, xiv, 67, 70, 75, 77, 119, 163, 164, 165
kashaf 11, 27, 55, 78, 79, 80, 83, 97, 98, 138, 160
kashaf ul qaboor 97, 138, 139
Kekulé, Friedrich August 10
khafi 33, 34
khilwat 49
khumaar 33
Kitaab al-Marqoom 143
koh-e-toor 49
Koran *see Qur'an*
kramin katibeen 96
Krishna 55, 156
kun 90, 145

L

la 150, 157
Lahore xii, 62, 75, 77, 119, 121, 163, 164
Lal Shahbaz Qalander 139
latifa ix, 29, 33, 80
latifa qalbi 80
Laws of Creation 17
Laws of Creativity 46
Light of Prophethood 156
Loh-o-Qalam 90, 163
Lot 25, 74, 100, 128

lungar xii, 70
Luqman 128

M

ma'arifa 52, 150
Maghrib 127
Mahabharata, Battle of 55
makaan 91
Mania 58, 59
Mark 50
Marx, Karl 11
Mary 49, 50, 79, 129
Maryam 128, 160
mashiat ix
masjid al-haram 51
masjid nabawi 156
Mecca 50, 51, 85, 128, 141, 160
Medina 156
Meditation iii, 3, 14, 31, 42, 45, 146, 161
Mental emptiness 14
meraj 50
microcosm 1, 2, 46
mo'min 46
Moses ix, x, 40, 49, 50, 55, 80, 128, 129, 137, 156, 161
Mosque of Mecca 51
Mosque of Medina 156
Muhammad xii, 40, 42, 46, 47, 50, 51, 52, 53, 55, 68, 69, 71, 72, 83, 84, 89, 95, 119, 125, 126, 129, 131, 156, 157, 158, 159, 160, 161, 163, 165
mullah 133, 134
Muraqaba of Void 151
muraqib 136, 146, 161
murshid xi, xii, 62, 75, 85, 126, 149, 161
mystery ix, 1, 33, 34

N

nafas 2, 25
nafs 33, 35, 148, 161
nafs vahida 148

nafsi 80
Nahjul Balagha 52, 163
nausea 59
Nazareth 50
nisbat 147, 156
noesis 43
nuqta dhat 6, 22, 90, 148
nur viii, 31, 32, 33, 40, 44, 46, 47, 52, 79, 80, 81, 90, 97, 126, 136, 137, 156, 157, 161
nur nabuwat 47, 156, 157

O

ORANGE LIGHT 121

P

paranoia 59, 118, 123, 124
Parasympathetic System 59
Parkinson's disease 59
Patanjali Maharishi 55
Patiala xii
People of the Book 129
Physics 2, 19, 29
PINK LIGHT 123, 124
pir xi, 161, 164
Point of Cognition 46
Point of Essence 22, 90, 148
prayer x, 3, 42, 50, 51, 52, 53, 76, 83, 94, 116, 125, 126, 127, 128, 129, 159
psychosis 57, 59

Q

Qalander Baba 83, 84, 89, 90
qalb 33, 148
qayam 53, 129
Qayam ul Salat 129
Qur'an viii, ix, x, 25, 41, 42, 43, 44, 46, 47, 48, 49, 50, 51, 52, 53, 68, 70, 71, 72, 79, 80, 92, 126, 128, 129, 130, 136, 138, 143, 145, 148, 157, 158, 159, 160, 162

Qutb 70

R

Ram 156
raqeeb 47
Realm of Allegory 152
RED LIGHT 75, 122, 123
remembrance 43, 51, 52, 53, 125, 128, 141, 159
revelation 7, 40, 48, 55, 78, 148, 153, 159, 160, 163
Roohani Daak xii
roya 26, 64
roya sadiqa 64
royet 158
ruh viii, ix, 2, 27, 28, 30, 33, 38, 81, 82, 147, 161
ruku 53
Rumi 15, 165

S

Sabi 45
Sadiqabad xii
sahib shahood 89
sajada 53
Sajjeen 143
salat 42, 51, 52, 53, 125, 126, 128, 129
Sanskrit 55
Satan 50, 160
Sauté Sarmadi 146
sayr 91, 92, 147, 148, 163
Sayr Afaaqi 148
Sayr Anfas 148
Schizophrenia 58, 59
Self vii, xiv, 1, 2, 3, 4, 6, 8, 22, 33, 37, 41, 46, 47, 52, 55, 57, 61, 74, 76, 83, 113, 122, 146, 148, 150, 152, 155, 156, 159, 161, 164
self-awareness 46, 47, 61
Shah Abdul Aziz Dehalvi 139
shahada 52, 129

shahood 88, 89, 90, 91, 147, 161
shariah 40
shaykh iii, vii, xi, xii, xiv, xv, 70, 71, 89, 102, 119, 120, 154, 155, 156, 159, 160, 161, 164, 165
Shaykh Maroof Karkhi 89
sifaat e'lahiya 147, 153
sifat ix
Siharanpur xii
silsila vii, 43, 161
Sinai 49, 80, 137
siraat musta'qeem 104
Soul vii, 2, 4, 24, 25, 26, 33, 34, 35, 36, 45, 46, 47, 55, 70, 80, 90, 130, 135, 136, 138, 139, 142, 155, 161
sphere of Heart 33, 34
sphere of sirr 34
sphere of Spirit 33, 34
spheres ix, 2, 33, 80, 81, 152
Spirit viii, ix, 2, 11, 23, 26, 27, 28, 30, 33, 34, 46, 50, 59, 73, 81, 82, 83, 86, 87, 88, 89, 92, 147, 161
spiritual brain 9, 11, 12, 24
Spiritual Laws 46
Spirituality x, xii, 45, 106, 126, 129, 136, 137, 162, 163, 164
Sufi orders 43, 164
Sufi Saints 43, 45, 70, 146, 160, 164
Sufism ix, 11, 22, 29, 38, 49, 51, 54, 77, 129, 145, 147, 148, 150, 151, 153, 155, 159, 160, 161, 165
Sunni xii, 160, 161
Sura 44, 45, 49, 51, 52, 79, 80, 92, 143, 157
Sura aal- imran 66 79
Sura Aeraaf 143
Sura Aeraaf 203 79
Sura Ankaboot 44
Sura Bani Israel 51

Sura Inaam 49
Sura Mulk 44
Sura Muzammil 51
Sura Najam 51
Sura Nur 52
Sura Rahman 45
Sura Shura 51, 52, 79, 157
Syed Ghauth Ali Shah 47, 139
Syed Shah Waliullah Muhadith
    Dehlevi 47
Sympathetic System 59, 144

T
tadjalli 30, 54, 80, 81, 82, 84, 90,
    129, 146, 147, 148, 157, 158
tafakkur vii
Tafheem 146, 147
Taleem Ghauthia 47
tarz-e-fikr vii, 156
tasarraf 12, 117
tassawar 100, 102
Tassawar Rasul 156
Tassawar Shaykh 97, 102, 154, 155
tawheed 40, 41, 52, 53, 149, 150
tawheed if'aali 149
Tazkira-e-Ghauthia 139
Telepathy xii, 11, 39, 98, 164
the Temple 49
Torah ix, 49, 161

U
Ultimate Reality 52
Unity 40, 41, 52, 53, 90, 149, 150
Unity of Being 90
Urdu xii, xiv, xv, 90, 92, 162, 163,
    164, 165
Urdu Daily Jung xii

V
vahii 40, 44, 79, 80, 81, 82, 83,
    157
Varood 77, 147
vijdan 33

VIOLET LIGHT 123

W
wahdat ul wajud 90
wahma 30
wali 96, 138, 159, 162
Waqar Yousuf Azeemi xii, xiii
weightlessness 74
Wisdom 42, 79, 80, 82, 146, 166
wudu 71, 116, 129

Y
Ya Hafeez'u 116
Ya'Haiyu Ya'Qayyumu 74, 125
YELLOW LIGHT 75, 120, 121
Yoga 55
yoga savitra 55

Z
Zachariah 49, 69, 70
zahir vii, 42, 45
zakat 51
ziarat 138
Zoroaster 156

ATTENTION: SCHOOLS, CORPORATIONS, SUFI ORGANIZATIONS, AND YOGA & MEDITATION INSTITUTES This and other books are available at quantity discounts with bulk purchase for educational, business or sales promotional use. For information, please write to

SALES DEPARTMENT
PLATO PUBLISHING, INC.
3262 WESTHEIMER RD 258
HOUSTON TX 77098

WORLD HEADQUARTERS OF THE SUFI ORDER OF
AZEEMIA

Markazi Muraqaba Hall
ST-2 Sector 4-C,K.D.A. Scheme No. 41
Surjani Town
Karachi-75850
Pakistan

The translator of this book, Syed Shahzad Reaz, is a student
of Shaykh Azeemi. He lives in Houston and can be reached
at :

muraqaba@sbcglobal.net